The Universal Doctrine

The Layman

RADIANT HEART PRESS

Milwaukee, Wisconsin

Published by
Radiant Heart Press
www.radiantheartpress.com

ISBN: 978159598-453-1
E-ISBN: 978159598-454-8
LCCN: 2016932253

Printed in the United States of America

*This book is dedicated to serious seekers only.
It is my sincere hope that sharing the lessons
from my spiritual journey will make
your own that much easier.*

CHAPTERS

Preface

Have you ever wondered what life is all about? Are we born to just die? What happens when we die? Is death the end? What is a saint's rapture? Does enlightenment really exist? What's behind the idea of Heaven and Hell found in practically every system of belief? What's it all about? The great perennial questions, what am I, who am I? Are there answers to these questions? Do we dare to ask? Do we dare to expect answers? What would you think if I said the answers are in this book. There's only one way to find out isn't there.

What would you do if something completely unsolicited happened to you, something way beyond your normal experiences in life, something even miraculous? How would you deal with it? What if this event were so outrageous, that even you would hesitate to tell anyone for fear that they would think you've gone insane, or at least a bit around the bend.

I had such an experience over forty years ago at the age of twenty-three. I feel as if I received all the esoteric truths that exist in this one split second interval of time. I'm still analyzing it to this day. I feel this experience explained life's mysteries to me from a very universal and nonjudgmental source, God if you will. I feel this same source has spoken to many people, in many cultures, throughout the history of man. I knew, when this event happened, I would have to share it with others on the path.

Now, after forty-four years, I'm ready, are you?

Introduction

I have to write this book as fictional. I do not wish to have to prove any of the events described in this writing actually occurred. There were friends I could use to testify as to the authenticity of some of these events. There is also published information proving that the personal experiences I describe in this book have occurred to others. I prefer for you to trust your own intuition as to the validity of the experiences I mention.

You will have to do your own research to confirm the validity of others having these experiences. If my friends do come forward and identify me as the author of this book, I will simply deny it. I do not want to attach a fallible human face to this work. Evidently, I was in the right place at the right time.

The messages conveyed in this book do not come from me. They do, however, come through me. I am really not capable of the beauty and vastness of knowledge that these messages contain. What I am writing about is not new to humanity. These experiences have happened to other people, past and present. I can promise you this. I am in no way embellishing these events. In fact, and I beg your forgiveness, I have to do the exact opposite. I myself have difficulty believing these events actually occurred, even though they happened to me.

Before you read any further, I must strongly warn you that after reading this book, you will quite probably never be the same person again. The entity you regard as yourself will lose some of its self-importance and with that, some of its ignorance. Your present goals in life will lose their importance as well. You will find these empty places filled with something much more gratifying however. I have to let you figure out what that "this" is as words do not suffice. I will try to use words to lead you to a place that is literally beyond words.

The place I'm talking about is beyond description. It's where you came from, and where you will end up. In Zen, it's described as a three-hundred-and-sixty-degree circle. You start out and end up back where you started, but you will know that place for the first time.

The Sufi saint says, "Die before you die, complete the circle before the circle is completed for you." In other words, go to it before it comes to you. Embrace the silence; it is our birthplace.

Anyone who can take this existence for granted, in my opinion, is sadly disconnected. I find myself in constant wonder. Please let me share with you what I have learned from a literally enlightening experience. I cannot say I am enlightened; I cannot say what I am. It is not my wish to proselytize. I wish to share with you the most amazing experience I have had in my life. Please, but only if you dare, read on.

I had some unusual or undefined experiences in my late teens. I did not know they were a bit out of the ordinary at the time. One was an overwhelming sense of well-being that lasted a few minutes. I remember thinking, "Boy, that was nice."

Another experience was the exact opposite, a very uncomfortable sensation causing my entire body to vibrate and sweat profusely. That event lasted a good twenty minutes. I was not able to stop it. At the time, I thought it must be a nervous breakdown, although I didn't have anything to be nervous about.

But the experience that occurred to me when I was twenty-three was by far the most powerful. In fact, it was explosive and lasted only seconds. The effects, however, have lasted a lifetime. It took me years to find out exactly what this experience was, since it happens to be extremely rare. It is said that this particular experience is indescribable.

There were other experiences to follow throughout my life but none anywhere near as powerful as that one. I feel as if I received all the esoteric truths that exist in this one split-second time interval. I'm still analyzing it to this day. I feel that this experience explained life's mysteries to me from a very universal and nonjudgmental source—God if you will. I feel this same source has spoken to many people, in many cultures, throughout the history of man. Now, over four decades, I feel I am ready to share this information with others on this path.

I follow no religion or organized belief system. I believe that we all have a built-in connection with what is called God by any other name. Why would it be any other way? Religions do serve as a valuable support system to many. All roads lead to Rome, as they say. My feeling is when we start out at birth, it's between us and God and when we die, it's between us and God. Please consider that information received from sources outside of your self will be filtered through the perceptions and egos of others (including this work, although I tried to keep it as pure as possible).

The purest information one can receive is found within. I want to show there is a direct connection between the self and the source of all knowledge. Now, in my late sixties, I want to share this information with others. I have known this as my most important purpose since this event occurred. It's not as though I think this knowledge will be lost with my death. On the contrary, I realize this knowledge always was and always will be. I may have a very simple "grassroots" approach for you, however.

I will use the word "God" to mean the creator of all things as a matter of convenience. My true feeling is "if a rose is a rose by any other name, then why not God?" So, God can be called whatever you like or your culture dictates. This entity is not partial to any belief system. How could it be? I believe one does not have to follow any particular path to reach this special place. Sometimes I will use the word "he" for convenience as well. This does not mean I believe God is male or that men are superior to women in any way.

In God's eyes, we are all equal. In addition, no system of beliefs is the one and only path. All of the belief systems have an element of truth at their core since the inspiration came from an identical source.

Survival dictated that we have a greater chance of success if we live and hunt in large packs. There is a natural feeling of security we humans feel in large numbers.

We are, by nature, a gregarious species. Religions certainly have their purpose. Most systems of belief were started by groups of people who took possession of another's inspiration and called it their own, better than anyone else's. They all proclaimed their way is the only way. Then they proceeded to contaminate the message of that special inspired one with the interpretations of their egos.

The sign of a worthy religion is when it embraces all other belief systems without judgment and without having to hang their sign out. There should be no prejudice. Interdenominational marriages should be allowed without question. This acceptance and respect for others can only engender positive qualities in people.

We are all born of the same seed. We are all truly one family. We need to see our likenesses in each other, not our differences. And, people from all races and belief systems have the ability to attain enlightenment. We should see a little bit of ourselves in everyone and everything. The smile of a child is universal. There are great truths in all of the Holy books, but the greatest, most pure truth, is found within oneself.

We all have a direct connection to this universal truth. The ocean and the drop contain the same properties has been said before. This truth can only be experienced directly and never learned through education. True knowledge is experiential. No one religion is the only way. All religions point in the same direction. The source of knowledge/truth is within each one of us.

People who have been touched by this universal truth throughout history come from many cultures. A blind, deaf mute could become touched by this "truth" after never hearing the name "Jesus."

I shall try to explain how this truth can be realized by anyone, and is in fact our birthright. Since most folks do not ever get to have the "experience," the next best thing is understanding, on a visceral level, in order to remove as much doubt as possible in your practice. It has to make perfect sense to you.

Some people choose the sectarian and/or doctrinaire path. I understand these paths are necessary to "get someone through the night." But these paths are second-hand knowledge. I want to share with you the secret of how to tap into the universal source of knowledge—commune with it, if you will.

I also wish to show there is a unifying factor, both in practice and in principle, at the nexus of all religions and systems of belief, as well as all of the art forms and other trance inducing activities.

I hope that sharing the knowledge and experience of my forty-plus years analyzing the profound and powerful spiritual experience that happened to me will help other serious seekers along this very special path. I have realized that this "truth" comes to every culture throughout the history of our existence as thinking and communicative human beings. God would never be prejudiced and give his/her/its knowledge to just one culture.

It is man who is prejudiced and attempts to make his way the only way. Throughout the history of mankind, these "religions" have sought to compel their beliefs on other cultures even with the use of force, if necessary. These religions all proclaim their messenger as the greatest. The truth is these messengers all tapped into the same source of energy for their inspirations. Who would be qualified to judge which teacher was greatest?

My message is to bring to light that all religions and systems of belief are all talking about the same thing, a unifying factor, a state of being. In fact, tapping into this same state of mind is what is immensely enjoyed by any accomplished artist, but to a lesser extent than that of the true seeker. I will explain why this is later in this writing.

If you can grasp the meaning and message in this book, you will have the key to the door to enlightenment. It does, however, have to make sense to you. One has to comprehend the incomprehensible. Then, to make matters even more complicated, once you figure it out, it's one thing to know the path; it's quite another to take it.

It has been said that no one can look into the eyes of God and live. I believe that you do live, but your ego slowly begins dying. This egoless state of being is the same in every human being. In Zen, it's called "no mind." In Christianity, it's called "a state of grace." In Buddhism, it's called "the clear light."

The event I experienced seems like it happened yesterday. I relive it every day, with every breath. I hope my story makes sense to you. What matters is whether you realize this as truth or fantasy. If you do realize my story is true, then the awakening I experienced may just as well have happened to you. This realization will come close to the actual experience, but will not replace it. It can serve as the greatest "ahha" moment one could ever have.

One has to enter that space for the true experience. The drawback of the type of instantaneous spiritual experience I had is you don't have the chance to acclimate. You find yourself stripped of your ego and in that sense "naked" to the world. There are some that have not survived with their sanity intact after such an event. I can certainly understand why. The benefit of the gradual path is that you get a chance to grow into your new spiritual self on an ongoing basis.

Thoughts to Consider

S ome people seem to be so inspired and happy and some people just suffer. There are some people who would steal the gold out of your teeth and others whose nature is altruistic.

Is this spiritual evolution? Would you rather be a poor artist who couldn't wait to get back to his/her painting in the morning or a rich person who can't sleep at night and lives with black emptiness?

It is said we are all looking for something, but we don't know what it is. In India, there is an expression that a man looking for enlightenment is like a man riding on an elephant looking for an elephant. We are always looking around the next corner for some kind of happiness and fulfillment. We are codependent on exterior stimuli for our happiness.

One can have all the money in the world and I guarantee you, there will still be this empty place inside. We go from one goal, feel temporary happiness, this fades, and then we create another goal and so on and on. That empty space is never really filled. I believe we are all spiritually blind. We know something is missing, but we don't know what it is. We must first discover exactly what it is we are missing.

Well, the answer, like the elephant, is right under our noses.

Think of thoughts as a radio playing between you and life. You will hear the radio over the other person's voice or the beautiful sound of the waterfall, or music playing.

Imagine no thoughts between you and your surrounding. The outside would become the same as the inside. There would be no separation between you and "IT." This is why artists feel so fulfilled with their music, painting, dancing, whatever their art form may be. Like Sufi dancers, they go beyond the thought process and become "one with the experience."

Please don't misunderstand—thoughts are useful, but not when they are used as a security blanket. We suffer isolation from this continuous inner dialogue. We cover up the silence. We block God out by trapping our spirit in a sphere of thoughts/self. We can't get into a vehicle without turning on the radio. We have to keep up the conversation. We have let the servant, our minds, a powerful bio-computer, become our master.

Why? You see, it's not the music, painting, dancing, skydiving, race car driving or even the most intimate of human actions that make us fulfilled...it's the state of mind/being these actions produce. That state of mind is selfless, that is without thoughts and at one with the moment.

Seekers discovered how to reproduce and maintain that state of mind without any exterior stimuli. Artists know how to tap into this energy and use it for purposes of creativity. They "get high" witnessing the energy flowing through them. For instance, musicians don't play their music; they listen to it being played, thereby becoming the "witness/calmful watcher/third eye."

This is like the eye of a cyclone or hurricane. Chaos/thoughts are all around but the center is still. This same design is also true for the consciousness. Mystics also know how to tap into that energy. The difference is mystics put a cap on it and let it build up. They don't "spend" the energy. They use it to launch the spirit into the cosmos and become one with it.

The Chinese *Book of Tea* calls it "the circulation of inner light." So light is energy is God. This is not a white light as is so often described; it's clear. It's the fabric holding all things in creation in place. It's the light in the projector of creation.

The only instrument capable of detecting this light is the human consciousness.

We are created in its image as a form of energy. We are given a spot of physical real estate within the grand infinite space called creation. We create our own world within this one. This is the source of suffering. Our separateness creates this disconnect. We have separated ourselves from this source of life giving energy.

There was a study done on an infant monkey separated from its social environment and isolated. In this study, the monkey is reintroduced to its natural social environment six months later. The monkey reacted with fear and violence. Even its physical stature was stunted.

So it is with us humans as well. The farther we are away from this source of energy, the more fear-based and dysfunctional our lives become. When we are able to merge with the center of this cyclone, we will be in the center of everything!

My Life Leading Up to This Event

'd like to give you a short background of myself so you can see my own personal/spiritual transformation. I was raised as a Catholic. I considered attending church a big bore and a chore. There was no love in my family, absolutely none. There was always arguing going on. I would retreat to the woods for the entire day by myself. There was peace there.

My parents finally divorced in my early teens. I was the oldest of three siblings. It was once said that my mother should not have had children. She was a very beautiful but narcissistic woman. I never received the love of a mother. I do not remember ever being held by her. OK, once. I was lying on her chest, my head over her shoulder. I must have been only months old.

I turned around to see a sock over a light bulb. My mother was darning a sock and that's how it was done. Even at that young age, I knew these two objects did not belong together, which is why I probably recall it so vividly. I don't know why but I have memories (picture image only) of events occurring very early on in my life.

Anyway, my sisters suffered in this way as well. My father was a nonexistent member of the family. He was always working. I felt a little like that monkey in the study, never loved, never held.

I developed a chip on my shoulder in my teenage years. This attitude continued into my early twenties. I was a bit of a tough guy, a recalcitrant and dissident youth, I'm sorry to say. The practice of judo and karate dovetailed well with this attitude. Of course, this façade was a way to protect the emotionally injured child within me.

Always, this inner conflict of personalities would vacillate. I always seemed to have what people called deep thoughts as a child. During my early childhood, before the age of ten, I would ask the elderly what it was like to get old, much to the embarrassment of my mother.

I wondered why people fought and argued, or how a seed magically became a plant, and how it seemed that sunlight shone inside my head when I lay down at the beach. And, even though raised in the country, where every kid had a gun including me, I only shot one animal—a rabbit. I could never shoot anything again.

From as far back as I can remember, I've always been analytical. I couldn't just play baseball. I had to calculate when the ball left the pitcher's hand and how long it took to get to me. Then I tried to see the path of the bat approach the ball in order to hit it. As you well know, this is an impossible task. I was lousy at baseball. I didn't make the team. I was very good at calisthenics, in fact winning the rope-climbing competition and setting the record for the physical fitness tests in a very large high school.

One day, while in high school gym class, I was playing baseball. The pitcher was the pitcher for our high school baseball team. Needless to say he was good. For some reason, when he wound up to throw the ball, something in me just decided to swing as hard as I could. And, that's exactly what I did. Finally, relying on my intuition, I hit a home run and even cracked the bat!

Most of my friends were musicians. I would wonder how they could play together for endless hours, cups of coffee never finished. What was it that intrigued them so? I envied them for their passion, but I was more interested in why. I realize now that my friends became my subjects of study. I probably could have played with them and eventually became a fairly good musician. After all, I was responsible for introducing them to jazz. They all became well-known jazz musicians. But, I needed to know why. My analytical self was still alive and well.

In my teenage years, adults would say "you're searching." I didn't know what they were talking about. I was always wondering about something. For instance, I never knew how someone just chose a profession, just chose a wife, and seemed to just know it was right. Around the age of twelve, my mother brought me to a therapist. I would ask him these questions. He, in turn, sent me to a specialist of some kind. I was diagnosed as "departmentalized." I don't know what this actually means beyond its face value, because it has no value to me. I never received any answers to my questions, of course.

I wondered about death, that black door at the end of life. I wondered what life was all about. I wondered why are we born to die, what is love, what is God? I wondered "who or what am I," where did I come from and where was I going? I wondered if these questions could actually have answers. I would observe my mind thinking like a radio playing. It would read signs, number plates, anything to keep it busy. I would try to not let it attach itself to these foolish actions to no avail. Looking back, I can see that I have always been a seeker.

I graduated from high school and attended several colleges although never got any degrees. I found, living on my own, that it was too difficult for me to work full-time to support myself, and attend college with no family support. My favorite subjects were philosophy, creative writing and earth sciences. Now, we get to the good stuff.

The Actual Experience

studied the martial arts for a short time prior to "the experience." I was fortunate to meet a master from Japan. He seemed to take a liking to me. One day he told me "if you really want to know San Chin, look for the space between your thoughts."

San Chin is a *kata* introduced to the monks by Bodhi Dharma, the first Zen Patriarch, to keep them in shape since their long meditation did not. This would indicate meditation as the focal point and the movements were employed to support it. In America, I see only the movements practiced. Anyway, I reasoned with myself that this was like a Zen Koan, such as "what is the sound of one hand clapping" or "does a falling tree make a noise in the forest if there is no one there to hear." I thought these questions were to get you to think. I was soon to discover quite the opposite.

One day, I told my friend, who was a black belt, what the master had said to me. He said we should try it. I never planned to actually try it. To actually sit there and look for a space between my thoughts sounded a bit absurd. The only exposure

I'd had to "meditation" had been the painful five minutes we kneeled in ceremonial bow position before karate class. I had no idea what meditation was.

My friend and I got together one evening to try out the Master's instructions. I lit the fireplace. I set out about six blankets each so our knees would not get sore. I sat on the left side of the fireplace and my friend sat on the right side. I dreaded the thought of sitting in the Zen ceremonial bow position, as it does become painful. And, I expected this to be a "competition" between the two of us.

I began to watch the course of each thought to see if there was any space in between them. It didn't take long to discover there wasn't any. One thought just rolled into the next one. There was only consecutive inner dialogue. I couldn't shut it off. I wondered if this was the way it had always been. I reasoned that when I was two days old or two weeks, or in the womb, it must have been quiet, without thought. There was no input to provide it with thought or images. So quiet must be in my distant memory. It had to be possible.

I carefully watched the beginning of each thought through to the end. Each thought came and went. After some time these thoughts seemed to lose their importance. I began to hear them as if they were someone else's.

I began to observe my entity objectively. I felt as though my body was just an outline. I now realize that I accidentally slipped into becoming what is called "the calmful watcher," "the third eye," or "the witness." I didn't even realize it.

The crackling fire seemed to come alive as if it had a personality. Then I noticed a ring in my left ear that was a different intensity than the ring in my right ear. I wondered how this could be. I again reasoned with myself, the left side of my body was towards the more solid center of the house and the right side towards the outside.

Oh, well, this seemed to satisfy me. I went back to the thought observation. The next thing I noticed was that my body was breathing by itself. As soon as I thought about it, I took over the breathing process. This took some effort. The ego has to control out of fear. I liked the sensation of witnessing my body breathe by itself. I was able to slip back into that state.

I was enjoying the feeling of watching my body breathing, like waves on the shore or a seagull's wings in flight, when I suddenly heard my heartbeat. It seemed very loud. My heartbeat no longer seemed external to my awareness. My awareness was now located inside my heart. The breathing and heartbeat were synchronized.

This process sounded like a symphony to me. This was a very quiet place. I felt like I was at a level of inner peace, produced by the quiet, I never knew existed. My consciousness bathed in it. I felt it was the first time in my life I got a chance to rest, to just be.

Think of being away for a very long time and the feeling you get when you finally get back home. There were sounds in this quiet. I was not making these sounds, nor was my body. I heard echoes in vacuums and sensed vibrations. I knew not the source. They were beautiful, beckoning sounds. I became lost in them.

These natural sounds took the place of my thoughts. My mind felt like it was floating in space. I was totally engaged in this wonderful, peaceful place. Then, I noticed a warm to hot feeling about the size of a peach pit in my spine just below the height of my navel. I thought how peculiar this sensation was. I had never felt anything like it before. It didn't feel uncomfortable, so I went back into the floating spacious feeling of quiet in my head. The warm/hot spot didn't get any hotter but grew in size to about an avocado.

At that point, I felt as if a hand gripped around my spine and was squeezing. Now it was uncomfortable. I felt I had to break this posture and leave this beautiful place. Then, and now, I ask your deepest understanding. Just before I was about to move, there was a loud sound like a clap, and all of my vertebrae cracked in succession, like a straight line of pool balls hit by the cue ball, from the base of my spine all the way into my head. I witnessed "the light." It was as if a car's halogen headlight was shining behind and through my eyes creating a sphere of light all around my head.

I experienced an indescribable feeling of love/ completion/compassion. I stood up and looked down at my friend. He looked up at me with tears streaming down his cheeks. He said "I know, I know." He stood up and we both hugged. Two macho men were now way beyond that type of mentality.

I stood on one leg and turned around 180 degrees in both directions with perfect balance. My body felt very strong. My body was infused with enormous energy. I could turn my wrists and hear my tendons crack and pop with uncommon strength. I was strong but nowhere near this strong.

I had no idea how much time had passed since I began this experiment of meditation with my friend. I now understand that my body never became uncomfortable in this nontraditional

American posture because it went into a sleep state. My consciousness stayed awake. My brain sent out chemicals to somewhat paralyze my muscles, as in sleep, so as not to injure oneself in the dream state.

I had no idea what happened to me. I wanted to talk to everyone I knew about it. I lost some friends. I became very close to others. Some thought of me as a teacher. I knew "the teacher" had come to me and/or through me.

Needless to say, this event changed my life forever. The sensation of "cosmic mind" would come and go even in my sleep over the next three months or so. Sleeping wasn't the same as before. I didn't really sleep. I would just sort of bask in this beautiful golden glow for three hours or so. There were very few dreams. That beautiful glow was my only interest.

These sensations would eventually fade although I would have "experiences" throughout the rest of my life. During the three months after this experience, I felt very spiritual, and—please excuse me—even holy. I felt as if the holy entity that others before me had experienced, had possessed my body with my permission (since I did not attempt to stop it). It was the most beautiful experience of my life. My senses seemed to be heightened substantially.

After this spiritual experience occurred, I wanted to know what it was exactly. Those were the days before Google existed, don't forget.

I called psychiatrists in the area. They all wanted to treat me as if there were something wrong. I asked them if they thought this extraordinary energy could be used to heal the sick. Now that I look back, I guess they just didn't believe me.

I spoke to several priests. They just wanted to recruit me into their church. I began to look into the works of philosophers, Dostoevsky, Kierkegaard, Nietzsche, and Kafka. I could not find anything that described my experience. The last place I would look was into religions.

But, at last, at a complete loss, I did. I found descriptions of some people who were considered saints that would go into states of rapture. Believe me, I am not a saint. If anything, I'm more like the wretch in the song *Amazing Grace*. But, the experience I stumbled upon could definitely be described as ecstasy, rapture, or a spiritual or religious experience.

What Happened to Me?

W hat about the explosion in my spine? What was that?

I was taking some courses at a local college. One evening, a Zen master gave a meditation lesson in the chapel. I went out of curiosity. A group of about fifteen students was present.

The Zen master wanted us all to sit in meditation. As we were meditating, one of the Zen monks clapped two pieces of wood together, making a very loud and sharp clap. I felt an electric shock wave shoot up my spine and practically lift me off the floor. Two currents of electricity crossed themselves back and forth in a zig-zag, just like the pictures in yoga show.

The monks and the Master seemed to know immediately what had happened to me. The Master came to me and wrapped his arms around me. I still had no idea what was going on. I wish they could have told me. He asked me what I practiced. I didn't know what to tell him. I used to practice karate. They couldn't speak English very well.

After this meeting, I read a little about Zen. I didn't run across anything that would describe that explosion in my spine which turned into the light experience I had.

Time passed. Some of my friends began to think of me as a spiritual teacher. Some friends simply lost contact with me. I was no longer the person they used to know. I liked this new entity enormously. There was this fairly constant glow of light and a love/compassion feeling that I wanted to be in forever. People really responded to this love.

There was a shift of consciousness that would happen by itself every so often. I will try to describe this shift. Once, when I was sleeping, enjoying this bathing in light, I felt like a beach ball of air held below the water that suddenly popped up above the ocean surface. Every molecule that I was expanded and merged into every molecule above the ocean surface. See how words fail? I hope this makes some sense to you. I feel foolish at times trying to describe it.

There was a flyer posted at the college I was attending announcing the arrival of some Indian yogis. I decided to see what these saffron-robed yogis had to offer. About ten or twelve students sat around cross legged. One yogi with a very intense stare sat before us. He seemed to look inside me. I could feel it.

The yogis asked if they could stay at my home when they were in the States. Of course, I agreed. This was the beginning of what would turn out to be the answer to all my questions. There were two yogis and their following who stayed with me at different times.

One was very strict, impersonal and down-right scary, like a sorcerer. The other was the exact opposite. He was so pleasant and loving. He stayed in my bedroom at night to sleep. I offered him my bed. I would sleep on the floor in a sleeping bag. He refused. He did not sleep. He stayed up in meditation all night long!

Once, when he had just arrived at my house, he seemed very tired. He asked to spend some time in a bedroom. He spent a less than an hour in there. When I saw him come out, his eyes were alight with energy. How had he accomplished this transition in such a short time?

We practiced meditation together every day. I was very impressed with the peaceful way about the yogis. They would sit in meditation for several hours. I could only stand about a half hour to forty-five minutes before I became uncomfortable. I was not able to enter the state where I had experienced the "light" with the cracking of my spine ever again. I would, however, get some rather strange sensations, such as a tingling in my solar plexus, sexual center, or throat area. These sensations corresponded exactly to the locations of charkas as defined in yoga.

Now I began to read everything I could about yoga. I finally found an exact description of what had happened to me. A book on Tantra Yoga described it as "when the aspirant becomes one with God." The description went on to say that the Kundalini is also called the "sleeping serpent," because of how it spirals up the spinal column when awakened. It is considered a dormant energy in man.

There I was, with no connection at all, ever, to this knowledge, and I experienced this amazing phenomenon. Please Google "Kundalini of the explosive kind." I would feel a bit braggadocio explaining it to you. Please keep in mind that this can happen to anyone. If you just happened to get your mind into this state for long enough and around your sexual peak, this could have happened. Of course, years of practice and preparation would help.

This amazing, phenomenal experience happened to me on my very first attempt "and I really didn't know what I was doing or what this phenomenon was"! From what research I have done, there are many different ways kundalini can be experienced, e.g., body spasms, tickling, vibrations, inner sounds, and increased sex drive.

Although there are some accounts of these manifestations of Kundalini in the Western hemisphere, there are very few. There are no accounts of the "explosive kind."

There has been one other testimony of the explosive kind of Kundalini on record. This was in India. Gopi Krishna writes about his own experience occurring on Christmas day in 1937. At least he knew what this phenomenon was since he was a yogi. I have only read excerpts of his writings. He states he went into what he calls twelve years of misery following the experience. I am not comparing myself with Gopi Krishna since he was a practicing and disciplined yogi. There are, however, many parallels with what he describes and my own experience. He has written numerous books on the subject of Kundalini.

Since the explosive kind of Kundalini is evidently very rare, I would not let this deter anyone from the overall physical and mental benefits associated with the practice of meditation, especially when accompanied by yoga postures. To me, the most important benefit is that of developing inner peace.

Perspective

Maybe the practice of handing down these ancient techniques from teacher to student by ear only is not only esoteric, but simply because no average person would believe them anyway.

That's why these pretexts are written in parable, something the populace can understand. Some of the events I experienced were so outrageous that I chose not to include them. Please don't think you're missing out on anything.

Ultimately the path leads you back to "average." You find it's perfectly fine to just be "average" and with a lot less exposure. This is also called the 360-degree circle in Zen. It's your perspective that's most important and that's what changes. You no longer take anything for granted. You realize "all this" is just too sophisticated to be an accident.

Prejudice

We can't look at other religions and categorize them as primitive or just not the correct way. This is nothing less than arrogance and ignorance. There are certainly aggressive actions taken by members of these religious groups that are primitive, since they are warlike.

Why do we act out of fear and not love? I believe that if Christ and Buddha met, they would meet as equals. Both received their information from the same universal source. We will all experience this sameness with the practice of meditation.

The pack theory has served the animal kingdom well. Human beings must go beyond that pack mentality. Could you eat a full-course meal in a room with three starving people? Sharing out of compassion is a sign of an evolved human soul.

Prejudice and ignorance allow people to practice "turn the page psychology." If we should see a photograph of a starving child, all we need to do is turn the page.

The one successful means of communication between people of different cultures is the heart. We are truly one family and we must come to realize this. We are the ones that will benefit by opening up our hearts to all.

Work on the Self

If we work on ourselves diligently, our sphere of energy will express itself. Like a pebble dropped into calm water, the rings of this energy will spread outward, affecting everything it touches. We must carefully see all of the traits we have acquired and, like a garden with weeds, remove the bad and nurture the good. We can then engender these positive traits to the children. They, in turn, will pass them on.

I want you to perform a simple experiment. Take, for instance, letting a motorist go while in traffic. Then watch them. Most will follow suit and let someone else go. It's as easy as that. We are truly one family.

With the practice of following, the teacher within each one of us comes to the realization that we are truly one family. We all must band together to let the bully minorities in control know that their behavior will not be tolerated in order to cure the world of its ills. Like thirty children in the first grade dominated by one bully, if the thirty children band together, the bully will be outnumbered and overpowered.

Our closest relative, the monkey, has the same structure to its society. The alpha monkey will hoard the group's possessions to show his dominance. But when he takes too much, the other monkeys get angry and band together to confront him. This is an actual scientific study. The alpha monkey ends up giving some of the possessions back.

Now think of the elephants. A mature female takes over the care of the entire herd. She will spend her remaining years putting the care of every member of this herd first and foremost until her death. What a beautiful sacrifice!

This is the pinnacle of social responsibility. We could learn volumes of important lessons from these examples. So we must take the responsibility for the spiritual evolution of man by working on our own personal spiritual evolution.

The Depression that Followed

The beginning of my downward spiral started within four months of my initial experience. I felt I was being tossed between heaven and hell. To say this euphoric experience had now become thoroughly traumatic would be an understatement. I was rejected by certain people. I was accused of dancing with the devil.

On the one hand, some people thought I was the second coming, and others envied my inspiration to the point of mentioning threatening bodily harm to me. And to add to this problem, the state of being—I can't call it a state of mind—did fade more and more after the first three months following this experience.

I became normal again. Human. No perfect pitch or extraordinary feelings of compassion/ love. My cosmic consciousness was being taken away from me. I plunged into the dark depths of depression. I felt God had betrayed me. I asked why.

The answer I received is "I took you there the first time, now you must find your way back on your own." I tried to copy the exact sequence of events that got me there the first time. My mind refused to obey. I could not concentrate enough. I became vacuumed up into daydreams. I mourned for my loss like a loss of someone extremely dear to me.

The ego is extremely powerful. It seemed to know it would cease to be if I went into that space again. I was afraid to lose my ego self. I stayed comfortably away from the line separating ego and God. The first time I experienced the light was an accident. Now, I would have to do it intentionally. That would be like stepping off a precipice and trusting you will not fall.

I tried to reject the powerful inclination I had towards this alternate life style. I tried to blend in with what was socially acceptable, sort of in between worlds. I couldn't relate to people. I was in possession of the greatest secret in the world, and I could not share it with anyone.

My secret was too farfetched for most people to believe. In my effort and struggle to fit in, I did the usual socially acceptable things, like attending parties, some drinking, and even the mild use of some recreational drugs. The latter was the zeitgeist of the 1960s, don't forget. But I was never able to feel a part of that social environment again.

I felt very isolated and alone with the burden of the knowledge I had received. I saw that everyone had an agenda. Existence was about survival, not love. I wanted everyone to see me, but no one did. I felt totally invisible to people because I was. I found people only saw in me what would potentially help them with their own idea of what they wished to be seen as and their own efforts at survival in life.

To add to my woes, I did not place any importance on becoming financially independent. My mind was constantly thinking about God. It was true for me that God is a very jealous suitor. I was stuck between two worlds, afraid to go in either direction. I realize now that I should have joined a monastery. After floundering between these two worlds for what seemed like forever, I realized that the need to be recognized or acknowledged by others lost its hold on me when I was about fifty years old. It just continued to wane away by itself. My jealous God won.

The world gradually lost its hold over me. I was no longer mesmerized. I could see the hidden agendas people harbored. Sometimes I would allow myself to be taken advantage of, hoping the other person would see me. Some would, but most could not. I could see how people were controlled by nature, just like the animal kingdom.

In a way, I felt I lost my innocence. I was no longer part of Shakespeare's play. In another way, I saw the majesty of God's creation all around me all of the time. And, there was no turning back. I would never be part of the play again.

Why Meditation?

Our minds are like radios playing on and on and on, and sometimes it can be the same recording, like hearing someone sing a song and you can't stop singing that song all morning. The mind can drive you crazy. The expression states "there is no such thing as sanity, only different levels of insanity."

The ego seeks to be constantly entertained. Sometimes the entertainment will not be healthy. Sometimes the mind races. It can seem like a bully as well. We cannot get into a vehicle without turning on the radio. We cannot be with someone without constantly covering up the silence with conversation. I'm sure we all want to just shut it off at times.

As human beings, we need peace and quiet. The mind is a powerful bio-computer. Once it has been programmed, reprogramming or deprogramming is quite an endeavor, but not impossible. The mind has become the master in most of us. Thoughts become a jail. There comes a time in the aspirant's life when he/she becomes feed up with the onslaught of thoughts in the bullying mind.

The more we practice watching the thoughts, the more we are capable of witnessing them, rather than becoming subject to them.

The very essence of our being desires peace. This peace is not just a relaxing experience like a vacation. This inner peace results in a total and complete transformation of consciousness. Through meditation, one gets closer and closer to the "original state" or "essence of being."

It can take a while before the elation is felt. This happens when the reconnection takes place. The essence of a being is the essence of creation. We choose music, dancing, painting, and so on, for that connection, but these are only temporary.

The ego will be a formidable opponent to you, protecting itself from what it sees as its annihilation. It will defiantly continue to attempt to define your environment in order to assert its control.

The ego is the actual guardian of this most beautiful original state of God/Light/Energy consciousness. There is only one way to accomplish this state of being and that is meditation/self-reflection to look within. We can become capable of discarding the negative thoughts before they take hold.

As you become more proficient in meditation, you begin to feel this quiet taking the place of your thoughts. You grow to prefer this quiet state of being more than that of any other. It is possible to go into a state deeper than sleep using meditation, since in sleep, the mind does not stop expending energy in its dream state.

The secret to this practice is to make a study of yourself. You must become totally objective to yourself. With the practice of meditation and the necessary self-observation it requires, there will come an ability to intercept emotions and thoughts before they can take hold. This ability will provide a new-found freedom from the negative thoughts we all have from time to time.

Most of us have experienced very special times when we naturally come to this state of being. I remember someone talking to me about his "special" experience and how it came about. He explained he was camping out with some friends in the wilderness. He took the canoe out in the nearby river by himself. He said he paddled for quite some time when suddenly the scenery seemed to transform itself. He said he felt every-thing "come together as if it were alive."

I knew exactly what he meant. With medita-tion, one becomes comfortable with the quiet this person experienced in the solitude of his adven-ture. Wonderful experiences, such as the one he explained, can become more and more a part of our lives with this practice.

To Shed Further Light

So, with all the varieties of entertainment in the world, you would never consider getting tired of them, would you? Eventually the games become all the same, just different. You're no longer a participant. There's something missing and you know it. You just don't know what "it" is. There's this bullying of thoughts in your head that will never be quiet. You do not have peace.

We don't have to keep the mind constantly chattering to entertain ourselves. We can deprogram ourselves. Artists can play all day long and not get bored. They are channeling this energy and experiencing a "high" from it. This is the same high and same energy experienced by saints, although not anywhere near as intense.

We have self-imposed our own exile from this healing energy by this constant inner chattering. This chattering creates a jail of thoughts separating us from this wonderful energy. We suffer from this isolation, then wither and die. We can try to convince ourselves that we are content, even happy. But, there is that constant emptiness within us that we are always trying to fill.

Channeling the energy our body produces is like watching the mercury rise in a thermometer. The spine is the stem, the ganglion impar, like the root system, the body like a mobile flower pot, the brain like an avocado seed (split down the middle the same way) and the hair like the silk on the top of a corn stalk. If we can learn to shut down the thought process for extended periods of time, this energy will liven up all of the centers in our body.

Don't think shutting down the mind will cause it to become less capable. Studies show that meditation increases the ability to concentrate, much like many artists accomplish in their practice.

Our energy comes up the spine, just like any other plant. Along the way, the energy is diverted to the centers for use. We've all felt that "pit in our stomach," that "chill up our spine," and that fullness of the heart when we feel love. When this energy reaches our brain, it is quickly consumed by that organ's hectic activity.

The brain uses most of the energy the body creates. The busier the mind, the more precious life force energy is wasted. The more thoughts racing through your head, the more ego, the greater the separation from this source. The racing mind will eventually be your demise, slow, but certain. The death will not be comfortable since this life usually ends in illness, physical and or mental.

It's when this energy can complete the entire journey from the base of the spine through the top of our heads that it can connect us with the cosmos again. This is when we will feel that connection and a great sense of completion. Once the mind becomes quiet enough, the consciousness can expand. The inside merges with the outside. The outside becomes an extension of the self. The self can realize eternity.

This is what the religions mean with the precept of "life everlasting." Until this point is reached, people can only "think" they have faith. Some say they "feel" they have faith. This may be a step closer. However, the only true knowledge is through direct experience.

When you give up your thoughts/security blanket, your spirit will take flight, the same as all of the great artists and saints throughout time. Once you are resolute in accomplishing this inner peace and quiet, you can never turn back. All of the hidden agendas of people and yes, even God's, will become quite apparent to you. "The game" will have nothing further to offer you.

When you arrive at this place of absolute inner peace and quiet, you will have realized the true self. You will perform all of the tasks you did before but with a twist. You will work for the joy of being. You will not want for anything since you already have more than you could ask for. You will not live to accumulate "stuff," although "stuff" may get accumulated.

Some people can experience the threshold of this "zone," if you will. They just don't realize it. Believe it or not, it can be taken for granted. It comes together when IT is realized. You have to be aware. The 360-degree circle described in Zen is complete. The soul has completed its journey.

We're all on that same journey. It's not like we will have "achieved" this state of being. It's like being on a journey and the destination time and place is not known. The "experience" just happens one day. With the practice of witnessing the self, the mind loses its hold over us and our spirits are set free.

There will be a time in your meditation practice when everything will become absolutely quiet. This is the moment when God will be listening to God. There are no words to describe this union of God and man.

You don't have to be a saint. The ego dominates our existence. It may be hard to believe but even the poorest have the same affliction. The scale must tilt in favor of the God/Light/Energy. It is said God accepts all who bring themselves before his alter. After one gets a taste of this oneness, it is certain it can never be used for any evil intent. This is because there is no opposite to God.

I have struggled over this with all of the violence in the world. My belief is this God/Light/ Energy is not just the energy that binds all things, but is in fact benevolent. The evil elements of the world are the manifestations of both individual and collective human thought.

So this universal God is pure conscious energy. In fact, it's like a brilliant light except it's clear. It can be sensed only when our awareness is at its peak. We must be running at close to 100%. When our being is one with the God/Light/ Energy, all of our senses are greatly magnified. We see everything differently. We will have perfect pitch, our vision will see every color enhanced, everything in the world will be animated (in fact it is, the one life force will be evident, it appears as a glow of light around everything), and we will become extra sensitive towards people and all living things. It is what is called Heavenly.

This light is all around us and it permeates everything. It is a pure, conscious energy, like a newborn. IT is the source of all life since IT is life. Therefore you might say that everything is alive and life is everywhere. IT makes no judgment, has no thoughts or sense of self. I feel foolish saying I believe IT does have a master plan, since it's so apparent. This God/Light/Energy is the basic building block of everything. The most basic of elements are still just particles. The actual God Particle is this clear light. This light is programmed by ITSELF and people. It then manifests into physical reality. It is the platform upon which everything else is built. The smallest particle has within it the instructions for a universe complete with intelligent life.

All of THIS did not happen by accident. There is definitely intent involved. We are a sphere of consciousness within this greater consciousness, like a bubble in the ocean, except there's no up and down. We are truly "created in Her-His-Its image."

The only thing that separates us from it is our sphere of thoughts that corrals our spirit. These thoughts are directly or indirectly concerned with ourselves, the ego. Artists are able to break through this barrier and tap into this limitless energy. They do it without knowing the process. They do it because they love the connection. When a musician breaks the ego barrier, this is what happens. They call it "in the groove" or "far out." The musician actually becomes the listener, not the player. He hears God playing his instrument.

That's why the music is way beyond the capabilities of the mind.

The same is true of artists of all kinds, but only after a certain degree of proficiency in their art is attained. Some musicians can develop perfect pitch because the sound is all they hear. Because the mind cannot successfully multi-task, the required concentration on the notes causes the consciousness to shift. It can switch from task to task, yes, but it can only deal with one task at a time.

You can't think and play, you can't think and dance, and you can't think and paint. You have to be the observer of your acts. You have to listen to yourself playing the music, watch yourself dancing, the painter watches the painting evolve, becoming lost in the act. The painting takes on a life of its own.

We must learn to see the world as our canvas, hear its sounds like a symphony. We live like prisoners in a cyclone of thoughts that separate us from the energy source. We soon wither and die because we cut ourselves off from the very source of energy that created us and all things.

It does not abandon us; we abandon it. All thoughts are manifestations of the ego. No ego, no self, equals no suffering, in fact, the kingdom of heaven is truly at hand.

Now, what does the sage do with this knowledge? Listen carefully, if you dare. When you meditate (see section on meditation instructions), you can accomplish this same "witness, calmful watcher, third eye," whatever you may call it, by achieving the following.

First, make the body totally calm. The mind will follow. You must give up trying to control. There is a dull light within your head. This is your consciousness, this is your control tower. Observe everything from this place. Let the breathing take place by itself. Simply hear each breath. Then hear the heartbeat, each one, then hear all of the natural sounds. The trick is to shift your attention from your thoughts to these natural sounds. The accomplished musician hears predominately only the music—no thoughts.

You can achieve this same state of being by listening only to the natural sounds, which are there all of the time. This symphony will beckon you into the universe. This universe is your new and real self. Come to the quiet place...and stay there.

Rest in this place. Maintain continuity of consciousness. This is the secret of the sages, the space between your thoughts is the portal to the universe/God. Bask in this pale light that you are. This light will merge with the light outside of it, the God/Light/Energy. It slowly becomes brighter, more intense. Visualizing light in the mind acts like a magnet attracting God/Light/Energy.

You can merge with this God/Light/Energy at your own pace when in corporeal form. You can feel the mind expanding outside of the parameter of your body, merging with the consciousness all around us (God/Light/Energy, also called the Akashic Record or Astral Plane, this is when you can sense eternity).

You will suddenly feel a shift in your perspective in your meditation. You will feel as if you are viewing yourself from the outside in rather than the other way around. This is when your being is no longer expending energy into the universe (dying), but receiving the energy from the universe into your being. This is the state of mind all of the artists and great thinkers revel in.

It is wonderful to experience how the mind addresses issues and comes up with solutions. It is even more impressive to receive intuitive flashes of information, not from the mind's deductive reasoning but, dare I say from God/Light/Energy. After death, the transition occurs too swiftly to remember your being. Become familiar with this spirit before the death of the body.

How to Meditate

How and why meditation works

Putting the mind in "park." We simply don't need to use the mind all of the time. Ninety percent of our thoughts are just meant to keep us company. This bio-computer requires an enormous amount of energy to create images and then attach a dialogue to them.

We create a drama which separates us from God/Light/ energy. We use it as a security blanket to keep ourselves company and keep our world small because the intellect cannot comprehend eternity and we fear that which we do not understand.

What we don't realize is that our true home is not the mind. Eternity, in fact, is our true home. When you give up your thoughts/security blanket, your spirit will take flight, the same as all of the great artists throughout time. With the practice of meditation, we don't need an art. All art forms are beautiful and gifts to humanity. In expressing an art form, the person becomes a conduit for creative energy. The artist, however, spends this energy. The body creates energy at a constant rate.

The difference with meditation is the energy is not spent, but circulated within. We can learn how to duplicate the artist's state of being, go beyond it and take this state of being with us constantly. There is no dependency on external stimuli. We are the only instrument required.

Find a place you can call your retreat. I use my attic. I have a bean bag with a cushion set up against a wall. My back is up against the wall with a small pillow placed between the wall and my lower back. I also think it's very important to use ear protection to block out external sounds. This takes the place of the cave or desert environment. Try to cross the legs and intertwine the hands if you find it comfortable enough. Comfort is an absolute necessity.

Now I'm going to share the secrets of the sages with you. This state of being can be accomplished by many different techniques. All of these techniques have the same identical result. They cause a suspension of the thought process. This is the "zone" all artists achieve and enjoy. All cultures have ways in which to achieve this state of being. The method involves studying yourself as an entity, objective consciousness, the calmful watcher, the third eye, the witness.

This is much like self-hypnosis. But this incorporates the study of God/Light/Energy.

Everything that exists is woven within a fabric of this God/Light/Energy the more energy you have, the happier you are. The harnessing of this energy results in "rapture." If I hadn't experience this personally, I would question its authenticity.

Start by visualizing the toes of the left foot. Visualize the cells like bubbles in soda. Visualize them losing their effervescence, ceasing movement, ceasing their vibration. Draw this sensation through the foot, lower leg, knee, thigh and stop at the base of the spine. Here, visualize an energy center, like a pebble dropped in a calm pool of water sending out rings. Visualize these rings coming back to the center.

Now go to the sexual center, same visualization.

Now the solar plexus, heart center and throat (Adam's apple).

Now the fingers of the left hand, hand, forearm, upper arm and back to the throat center.

Now the fingers of the right hand, hand, forearm, upper arm and back to the throat center.

Do an overall scan of the body, see the network of nerves like roads on a map and cease their vibrations. Bring your awareness up into the cavern of your mind. Sense that which senses the senses.

The body is now only a shell, an outline. All energy expenditure is stopped. There must not be any facial expression. Even the eyes must stop moving.

Go bravely into the depths of the silence. Maintain this state of being for as long as possible without discomfort. You will feel when the energy starts to build up. There are different sensations for everybody. Some of you will actually feel the yogic centers start to vibrate. There could be waves of energy sweeping over your head as if some of your hair starts to stand up and cracking of the spine is not uncommon (although this should not be forced as it could cause injury).

The body is especially sensitive after meditation because all of the nerves are slightly swollen. It is wise not to do anything strenuous or involving stretching for at least half an hour.

Imagine there is a battery at the base of your spine (the ganglion impar). This battery stores energy obtained from everything you eat and the earth's bio magnetic field. It then supplies electricity to the centers as depicted above and in Yoga. These centers do exist. See the centers like light bulbs using the energy from the battery. As you unscrew each light bulb by deactivating that center, the last bulb on the top receives all the energy. It's really that simple.

There is a natural light in everyone's head we have taken for granted and no longer notice. Focus on this light. It will look similar to a TV screen in between stations. That "noise" showing on the TV screen is actually "noise" from the universe. In fact, it is seeing the same light/dark – yin/yang that encompasses everything.

Let your consciousness bathe in this light as if you were lying in the sun. Focusing on this light inhibits the mind from creating images. You see the mind creates images first then attaches a dialog to them and "voila" you are in a dream within a dream.

WAKE UP! At this point, mantra is very important. One ruled thought disciplines all of the mind's unruled thoughts. The most powerful mantra is *Ham-so*, pronounced hung, as your body inhales, and soooooo, as your body exhales. In Sanskrit, it means "I am one with Spirit". This mantra is actually the sound of the breath itself.

Eventually, with practice, you will hear your own breathing say the mantra. You will not have to say the mantra to yourself. Your mind will be completely quiet and used only when you want to use it.

In our meditation, we have a choice of which to listen to, ourselves (or some other manmade sound) or the universe. So, fixation on the light and fixation on the mantra (or better still, the natural sounds) inhibits the mind from wandering and creating dreams which divert your connection to the cosmos = God/Light/Energy.

Listen to the natural sounds, the ring in the ears, the heartbeat, etc. These sounds will lead you to other sounds, sounds that your body/mind is not making. These sounds are produced by the cosmos = God/Light/Energy. This is how you can enter it.

Lock into the image of light and the natural sounds only. You will hear the wind, crickets in the forest at night, rushing water, waterfalls and other wonderful sounds. These sounds will take you back to when you first heard them, in your mother's womb, and even before. This pureness of consciousness is a memory within each one of us.

Learn to make this space within your mind a very peaceful and quiet place. Let the body breathe by itself, just witness. It is especially important to not expect anything. This is the ego and everyone has one. To have an ego doesn't mean one is a braggadocio; it just means your mind is filled with thoughts. Those thoughts are about you whether directly or indirectly.

It could take years for you to have any unique experiences. That's okay. You cannot make anything happen. It will happen by itself. Just learn to enjoy the peace and quiet. This is where these extraordinary and wonderful experiences with come from. When the spirit is able to "just be", listening to the natural sounds and focusing on the inner light will become our communal with God. Being able to maintain this state reduces the self/ego and increases the God/Light/Energy. The witness that we are is never lost nor can it die. Knowing this is one thing; realizing it is quite another.

We need to go beyond the thinking thoughts/mind, which serve the self and to the actual source of this energy to know the true self.

And, only one more thing (for now). During meditation, curl the tongue up between the fleshy part and the hard palate on the roof of your mouth. You will find a little pocket there. This is called *kecheri mudra*. It is used to reflect energy back into the body.

The more you meditate, the more you will look forward to it. Vacations are nice for relaxing and regenerating, but what about an ancient technique for balancing the body's energy and quieting the "wild horse within." We have truly allowed the servant to become the master. Learn to make the most peaceful place you know of right inside your mind.

When the mind becomes totally quiet, the inside will merge with the outside of your body. There will be a oneness you will experience. The drop will become one with the ocean. The Sufi saint says "die before you die, complete the circle before it is completed for you." Only spirit can know Spirit and only through experience, not through accumulated knowledge.

You will know when your practice of meditation is taking root. You will subconsciously avoid all chaotic environments. You will begin to hear sounds and see things like never before. The sound your tires make on the pavement will be musical; the bubbles in a bottle of wine will be viewed as art. Many more of the wonderful events that go on constantly all around you will become your source of entertainment and joy.

So learn to just be. Sit quietly, let the breathing take place by itself. Bask in the light within your head. Give yourself a break. JUST BE. I'm not saying to discard the thinking mind. It certainly serves a purpose. I'm saying we must break our dependency on the thinking mind like any addiction. We must learn to reconnect with that part of our nature that creates the thoughts. When we do make this reconnection, there will be a sense of expansive inner peace and quiet that we will relish with our whole heart and soul to the exclusion of all other states of being.

Note: I believe this method of meditation can be used to heal. With the assistance of hypnosis, a person with an illness can be taken into an advanced state of meditation. If the subject can be assisted by the hypnosis to maintain a focus on the inner light and sounds for an extended period of time, the natural energy will build up. This energy will then reinforce the immune system and balance the body's energy field which should defeat even the most stubborn of illnesses. It would be of extreme advantage to perform this practice on a daily basis.

The Practice of Repetition
in All Belief Systems

When I was a child, attending catechism was required as a member of the Catholic church. There I was told, "God is everywhere." I thought about the meaning of this statement. I was dumbfounded by it.

After my experience, I realize what that statement means. Everything is the mind/energy of God. We reside in that mind/energy. We are given a small piece of real estate for a short period of time. We are like a bottle submerged in this space. The thoughts/ego fill the space inside the bottle. This bottle separates us from the outside God/Light/Energy.

Quieting the thoughts/ego allows the space outside to enter. This energy is God. The phenomenon I experienced did prove to me that all religions do teach this path of quieting the mind with different techniques. These similar techniques are used to displace the thought process. The practice of any art form achieves the same thing. Tantra Yoga makes an actual science of this.

All belief systems use the same technique to achieve the state of being. I will try to clarify these unifying factors for you. That technique is the use of repetition. Christians use the name of Jesus, Catholics use *Kyrie Elision* or counting the rosary beads, Muslims repeat the name of Allah, Buddhists repeat the mantra "*Om mani padme hum*", and in Hinduism, one of the mantras is *Rama, Rama*. There is also the practice of the physically repetitious *kow-tow* by the Muslims, the whirling Dervishes, or the twirling dance of the Sufis.

Please ask yourself why there is this practice of repetition common to all of these systems of belief. I will tell you it is a method used to suspend the thought process. The purpose of these practices is to achieve the union of the inner spirit and the spirit outside which is God. The only obstacle that separates the two is the thoughts/ego. When there are no more thoughts, there will be no more ego. The thoughts/ego is our own self-created jail to our spirit and the cause of all our suffering.

Traps on the Path

While meditating, revelations will come. We will be assaulted with wonderful and creative ideas, solutions for problems, etc. This is shown in Tibetan Buddhism as the serpent devouring its own tail. This can go on forever. We must shut this process off and go beyond it. We must relearn to be quiet.

There is also the manifestation of paranormal and spiritual experiences. Since we must stop looking around the corner for "more" these experiences must also be simply observed. Like thoughts, let them come and go. Desire is a huge trap. Realize we are already complete. Just being is where the bliss is.

Also, when you get deeper into mediation, you can hear all of the natural sounds. The ego will still attempt to drown out reality by mimicking those sounds. To achieve the clarity the mimicking must be bypassed. Then one will be on the threshold of oneness!

We all naturally gravitate back to our starting place, drawn to the light. When first starting the practice of meditation, the mind will still try to trick you. It will come up with epiphanies that will astound you. You will feel compelled to stop and write these revelations down. This is a huge pitfall. The ego is tricking you and preventing its silencing. You must ignore these entreaties from the ego, no matter how impressive they sound.

I do realize this writing is the documentation of all of the realizations I have experienced. My intent is to give them to those that seek this true path. This is a compilation of the realizations I've had over the years of my practice. I have not allowed these impediments to intrude on my practice of meditation for at least the past decade now. This writing is my first and it will be my last.

Reward and Punishment

We are born with a mind that is relatively pure. I say relatively because we are born hardwired for survival. The spirit does carry over the energy from previous lifetimes. Eventually, this relatively pure mind is largely programmed by its environment. This spirit within each of us listens to and becomes directed by the content of these acquired thoughts. We are given a small piece of God's real estate (pure consciousness) to use for a period of time.

The only thing that separates us from the pure and eternal spirit/consciousness is that circle of thoughts that surrounds us. God gets to peek out from the experiences of every living creature in existence. God does not direct or intervene.

Humans have lived many lifetimes. How does harm come to innocent babies? There are no innocent babies. These souls have lived previous lives. It is not as if God punishes or rewards us, it is because we create our own world with our own energy within this sphere of energy, as if we are projectors making images on a screen.

There is no debit and credit column kept. It's not an eye for an eye or a tooth for a tooth. I have long tried to understand the meaning of "we will reap what we sow" and "karma." I do not think a reward and punishment system is at work here, at least in an eye-for-an-eye sense. If that were the case, Christ would never have been nailed to the cross and Gandhi would never have been shot. This is certainly not the energy they manifested. I believe Christ and Gandhi truly gave up their lives in order to complete their missions here on earth. Their spirits knew this sacrifice was necessary.

We are dealt a hand of cards, if you will. We have to learn to make the best of that hand. I do feel that those who are on the path are given the tools to deal with whatever situations in life they are faced with. Those who seem to have received all of the material gifts imaginable may live in a very dark place, isolated and unable to sleep. They may have the largest home along with several vacation homes. If their energy is devoted to acquiring material things, then this surely means they are creating and maintaining a persona if you will.

The real person gets lost in the avatar we create. The more "stuff" we acquire the greater the energy expenditure. This energy expenditure is often more than our bodies produce. This will eventually cause physical and/or mental illness.

People with big egos cannot see the magic of the world around them. They create drama out of boredom. Of course, creating this drama makes them the center of attention. A person with less ego is more spiritual. This person does not need to create drama. He/she is already overwhelmed at the mystery of creation.

Spiritual persons will find more beauty in their own ordinary backyard than these worldly people can see on their own private tropical island. These people will see the island as just another material acquisition. These people will undoubtedly write their own obituary column to, as they did in life, to make themselves look as good as possible. Wealth can be a great burden. A wealthy person may never know who his real friends are. Of course this does not mean all of the wealthy are condemned to misery.

People who expend their total energy trying to acquire material goods, whether achieved or not, are missing the real prize. Those that may have received little can find bliss in the streams of sunlight passing through the limbs of a tree, the prismatic play of light through a wine glass reflected on a tabletop or frost on a window pane.

Some people are in such a hurry that they never see these little miracles. Cast your bread upon the waters and it shall return, you reap what you sow, and the principle of Karma are all in accordance in this sense. This does not mean only good things will happen to good people and only bad will happen to the bad people. It does mean that good people will be able to experience love, joy and compassion. Those souls that are filled with ego will not be able to experience these simple and most beautiful joys. They are more likely to harbor ill will, jealousy and the judging of others.

So, the principle of "you reap what you sow" and "karma" are very difficult to comprehend, let alone to explain. Sometimes it will seem like we are treated unfairly in life. We may experience a betrayal, a financial loss, etc. In reality, these events can turn into exactly what we wanted and needed in order to experience spiritual growth.

We are surrounded by our teachers. Every episode of life is a lesson. We can learn to see ourselves through this reflection. It is important that we observe our reflection and not identify with it. We must learn to not identify with anything. This allows our spiritual evolution. To cling to an identity is to stagnate and to stagnate is to die.

Stages of Death

Meditation simulates the stages of death. When a person dies, he/she is protected from the event and the pain of the process by a form of shock. The spirit is much too wise to suffer any pain over a certain threshold of severity. The mind goes into a dream state. As the mind/spirit dreams and there is no longer any exterior stimuli to reinforce the dreams, the dreams become fragmented. The spirit soon recognizes something is wrong.

If this spirit has not been exposed to the comfort of true and complete inner peace during its lifetime, it will recoil in fear at the sudden realization of what it perceives as isolation. As the dreams fade, the spirit will forget its position in life, its name and even its gender. The spirit finally is cleansed of any ego content.

Like a seed that has gone dormant, it becomes re-energized to re-emerge into life. It is ready to be born again into the physical world. If the spirit has been exposed to the feeling of total inner peace/quiet, it will embrace the light. This light will feel like the home you've missed so terribly.

We have all been seeking this missing part of us without knowing it. Throughout our lives we have all been seeking something we do not understand. We know something is missing but "we can't define it." We are all spiritually blind. Meditation is also the practice of letting one's sense of self (ego) go. We discover we are an energy form that is in a state of constant metamorphosis.

Most people cling to what I've called "crystallized consciousness." People hold onto what they think they are. This is a burden since it requires a great expense of energy which ultimately wasted. The path can only be followed by letting go of this conception of what we think we are. Following the path is innate in each of us. Deductive reasoning is a process of the ego. The path to home is intuitive.

Unusual Experiences

I was in the act of simply leaving my apartment one day when I stopped as if frozen in time and space. I looked in front of me and felt that the outside of me was the same as the inside of me. I felt I was the outside, too. This feeling lasted for about fifteen seconds. I could not comprehend it but I did experience it, if that makes any sense.

Now, over forty years later, science through quantum mechanics, is investigating the possibility of the universe being a living entity. It is, and this is called pantheism.

I remember walking with a friend down to the river near my house once. I was in this state. He felt it. There were two stone pillars. My friend sat on one and I sat on the other in silence. There was no need for communication. We were one. The river felt like an open artery in the earth's crust. We could feel it. I could feel the power, depth, speed and breadth of the river. This was ecstatic. He said later that he never knew I was his teacher. I told him I wasn't, but IT was, his as well as mine.

A friend of mine was leaving my house. It was wintertime. I thought I might just go out with her for a minute or so to bid her farewell. I had pajama bottoms on, a tee shirt and my slippers. When we walked outside, the conversation went on a bit longer than I figured. Then this very bizarre physical phenomenon occurred. I felt a source of heat emanating from my stomach just below my navel area. It was a little smaller than a soccer ball. It actually felt like flames flickering. This heat warmed my whole body. My friend was standing about five feet away. She asked me if I was cold. I told her I was not. She said "I know, I can feel your body heat from here".

Note: I now know this phenomenon is called "vital heat." It is practiced by the monks in the Himalayas. It is said some monks can dry a wet cotton blanket simply with their body heat and this takes place in subzero temperatures! This practice has been researched by Dr. Herbert Benson, author of *The Relaxation Response* (and other books).

Two of my friends and I were in meditation. I began to feel my heart start to pound in my chest quite loudly. At the same time I could hear the heartbeats of my two friends. ALL THREE OF US HAD ONE HEARTBEAT! Our heartbeats were synchronized. One of my friends asked, "Are our hearts beating in unison"?

I answered, "Why did you have to ask?"

Note: Many years later, I was watching a science program about a study of how this can happen. They took a cell from three different hearts and placed them on a Petri dish in a laboratory. The heart cells all beat individually. When the heart cells were brought into proximity with each other, all three started to beat simultaneously! This study also showed how two people that have a powerful chemistry attraction sometimes called love can actually have their hearts beat in unison as well.

Scientists have recently released the results of a study proving how birds that flock together seem to fly as one entity. Their research, so they say, proves that a bird is able to process the direction a neighboring bird is going to travel in and follow that direction. I believe that if the scientists can somehow check the heartbeats of each bird in the flock, they would discover that the heartbeats are in unison. These birds are flying as one entity. This oneness is universal with all living creatures.

Music: I had very little musical ability, yet I played the flute in a chapel with my own echo. I would play a note and when it reflected off the back of the chapel and came back I would play off that note. It was as if there were two flutists playing. I had a very accomplished jazz musician friend. He was trying to remember a long and difficult horn solo without success. I just scatted it off vocally to his amazement (and mine). I could sing and hear my voice's echoes bounce off the corners of the room.

I believe I gained perfect pitch for this period of time. I could tune a guitar effortlessly. It had always been a chore. Now I could "see" the vibrations synchronize in my mind. I felt in touch with the world/spirit around me and those that were with me, somehow, felt the same sensation. It was as if I was surrounded inside and out by God if you will. Spirit met with spirit, oneness.

I was running at my fastest speed down a path in the park near my house in the black of night, just for the fun of it. I felt like a meteor in the universe. In an instant, I found myself sitting on the ground and quite bewildered. I felt my lower chest area and noticed a bump in my skin all across the front. I was not in pain; there was no blood loss. I got right up to investigate and then noticed a chain had been placed across some posts since the park was closed. I had just run into that chain at full speed and was completely uninjured with the exception of a small welt and red mark.

Some call it divine intervention. I was on a highway in the early morning on a weekend. Since this was a vacation area, there was no traffic on the road this Saturday. This highway had two lanes on either side of a center divide, four lanes in total. This center divide had some plantings giving it a very natural setting. I had to take a left turn, which required me to take an exit which then intersected perpendicular with the highway. I stopped at the red light. When the light turned green, a feeling of confusion came over me. I was having a difficult time accelerating to cross the four-lane highway. I felt completely foolish. Luckily, there was no traffic.

I inched across the first two lanes slowly even though I had the green light. I didn't know why I just didn't step on the gas and continue on my way. I wasn't afraid; I just couldn't seem to move. As I approached the center divide I, of course, looked to my right for oncoming traffic even though they had the red light! A black pickup truck went flying through this red light. The speed limit was fifty miles per hour. This guy, on his cell phone, was definitely doing sixty-five miles per hour. He flew through his red light without even a glance in my direction. I did not exaggerate this event. As far as I'm concerned, divine intervention saved my life. This is one of the many rewards of "being in touch" with the consciousness/God all around us. This event happened just recently.

I was walking with a good friend in the park next to my house. We were just coming up an embankment to the road. It was dark out. There were some street lights. I saw a car coming around a corner in the distance. I saw an eerie glow around the car. It was as if the car was governed by an evil presence. I told my friend to crouch down until the car passed. He shrugged off my suggestion with a bravado. I insisted with entreaty that he crouch down and so he reluctantly did. The car passed us. It was full of young men listening to loud music. It was easy to sense the raucous intent. I believe we avoided an altercation by literally keeping our heads down.

Little Miracles

1 was with a friend walking to the beach. We had just left our car. We came upon a group of women, probably five or six, gathered around a very large boulder by the side of the walkway to the beach. There was definitely some grave concern in their conversation. As my friend and I approached, I noticed a young child, probably three or four, sitting on top of the huge boulder. There was a crevasse splitting the boulder where it had broken apart over time.

I asked what the problem was. Someone explained that the child had pressed her foot into this crevasse and now it was stuck in an opening below. No one could pull it out. Her poor foot was red with the attempts. They said someone went to get help. I walked up to the child and asked her what had happened.

Being a red-blooded female, she went right into a detailed explanation of the sequence of events. I didn't realize it at the time, but I had my right hand wrapped around her lower leg. As she talked, without any premeditation, I abruptly yanked her foot right out of the crevasse. You should have seen the look of wonder on her face.

I said, "Here's your foot back, sweetie. Now go enjoy the beach." Then my friend and I walked away.

When we were about ten or fifteen feet away, I heard one of the women say, "He must be a doctor; he knew exactly what he was doing."

The truth is I am not a doctor and I didn't have the slightest idea what I was going to do. The act was completely unplanned and completely intuitive. The spirit moved me. This is what being connected can achieve. What a beautiful memory.

* * * * *

I lived on one side of a fairly large river, which separated two cities. There was a bridge going across that had a bend in it when it reached to opposite bank. There was always three or four accidents a year involving drivers who underestimated the severity of the curve.

One evening, I heard the familiar sound of a loud crunch and shattering glass. I ran out and saw a car off the side of the road. I saw that it had sideswiped the telephone pole. Four or five girls of college age stood outside the vehicle. None of them appeared to be hurt. They all had their hands covering their mouths with a look of terror on their faces. Another girl was on the ground screaming, "I can't walk. I'm paralyzed from my waist down!" over and over again.

None of the girls were helping her. My spirit took over. I knelt down beside the girl and placed her head on my lap. I began to speak calmly to her. The spirit said, "I know you think you are hurt. You've been involved in a bad accident. Think of this like a bad dream. Tomorrow morning, you will wake up and remember this as just a bad dream. You are not hurt. You are fine. Now let's get up off this ground so you can go home."

I assisted her as she raised her upper body and without hesitation, we both stood up. The other girls all gasped as if this was some sort of miracle. How did I know she was not paralyzed? The truth is, I did not know. The spirit did. And yes, the rescue squad did eventually show up. I just went home and back to bed.

* * * * *

These two scenarios are just examples. I didn't think anything of these events back then, just took them for granted. Many more of these events occurred throughout my life where the outcomes were completely beyond my scope of knowledge, yet the spirit would provide me with the solutions. This connection is available to us all. I consider them "little miracles."

* * * * *

I was sitting on a dock with a dear friend in upstate New York on the shore of a very large lake with trees all around its edges. The day was perfect—warm, sunny, with floating clouds and small waves lapping up on shore. We were sitting in silence absorbed in the beauty before us.

Then, in an instant, everything transformed into a living, vibrant energy with hues of color surrounding the trees, water and clouds. The energy encompassing the entire view was a living entity. It was God making him/herself known and visible.

The scene was already postcard beautiful, when it suddenly became so enhanced we marveled. It was as if I had been seeing in black and white my entire life until that moment. This transformation lasted three or four seconds at most. I stood up and asked my friend if she had seen it. And she responded "yes."

I said, "You were going to keep it to yourself, weren't you?"

We witnessed this miracle together and yet, never mentioned it again to each other. In our youth, we took this for granted.

* * * * *

This little story shows just what the Kundalini energy is capable of. Another friend asked me if I wanted to visit an old friend of his. He said there were some guys who were going over there to hang out. I said, "Sure, let's go."

On the way, he told me about his friend's cat. He said the cat loved to play "cat and hand." I asked him what he meant and he explained that if you held your hand pointed upwards in front of the cat, the cat would pounce on it. He said no one had ever beaten the cat.

We arrived at the house and went in. There was a media room in the basement with a very large sectional couch. I had forgotten all about the "cat and hand" story. We were just talking about stuff and having a few beers.

The cat must have known I was new to the crowd. She came up and sat directly in front of me. My friend said she was challenging me. He reminded me to hold my hand in front of her about a foot away. So, I did just that. The cat nonchalantly looked at my hand and then she took her pounce posture.

She waited calmly, then suddenly pounced. I pulled my hand away in a nick of time. I had beaten the cat! She ran to the other side of the room, sat still and looked at me. Everyone was watching. Half a dozen guys were there.

The cat just stared at me. What a smart animal. She sat there for a few minutes then strode over to me again. She took her position. I slowly placed my hand in front of her again. She waited, feeling her ground for a minute or so. Then, like lightning, she struck. Again I was able to pull my hand out of her reach. This time the cat took off and ran across the top of the sectional couch and into the adjacent room.

She did not come out of that room for the rest of our visit. This is a true story. We all had a great laugh at how upset she was. Someone finally beat the cat! I think back in wonder now. How could a human being ever be faster than a cat, especially when the cat made the first move? This is truly an impossible feat for any human. This speaks loudly for the power of the energy of Kundalini.

Dreams

I dreamed there was a violent storm so powerful that it threatened to pull my house off its foundation and up into the sky. In my dream, I thought the only way to face it was to go outside. I slowly opened the front door and peaked outside. I saw a dark, nebulous, putrid, green wind swirling around my house and pulling me outside.

As I took a few steps outside, I felt my strength draining and I began to fall to the ground. The earth began to drain my body of its energy. I felt I was slowly dying as the cells of my body began melting into the earth.

A little voice seemed to tell me to push up off the earth. I said I had no strength. The voice said to use whatever strength I had. I tried to push up. The more I tried to push, the greater my strength grew.

When I finally was able to stand, the storm had passed. A star was just above the horizon and the glow of the morning sun was beginning to light up the sky, stars still visible. I looked over at the bank of the hill that actually existed in real life.

There were three lilies in full bloom. I never knew what the significance of lilies meant at

Catholic funerals. Maybe the spirit spoke to me in symbols I'd be familiar with. As the flowers most often associated with funerals, lilies symbolize that the soul of the departed has received restored innocence after death.

I believe this dream was a confirmation of my rebirth.

* * * * *

I formed a short-term business venture with someone I thought was a friend did not turn out well. I had many childhood memories with him and his brother. Our fathers were lifelong best friends. Both had now passed on. Although there was a period of time when we went our separate ways, when we reconnected, it was as if we never lost touch.

In this business, I invested the startup capital. In a dream, I saw my friend. He was sitting in a crouched position, his knees up to his chest and his arms wrapped around them. He was attached to a wall and suspended halfway up. I came closer to see how this could be. As I approached, I noticed something even more peculiar. His feet were cloven! I was receiving a warning that the person I thought of as a friend had a hidden agenda. And, as it turned out, he certainly did.

Vision

I came home from work one day and walked toward my front door. I could see the sun going down. I went over to the side of my house so I could get a better view of this rather beautiful sunset. When I looked at the clouds and the colors, the scene instantly transformed to something surreal.

From the bottom of a cloud to the left of my view, a white-gloved hand dripped down. The ring finger was missing. I knew what this meant.

The woman I thought of as my mate for life was not to be.

A Short Stint in the
Mental Health Field

After my Kundalini experience, my intuition was at a peak, and a very high one at that. I could not tell verbatim what people were thinking, but I knew the basic content. Two women from the yoga circle got the idea that I could help people with their personal problems. These people were apprised of my abilities to able to intuitively see into the dynamics of behavioral issues, including the negative ones, of course. These two women set up appointments with people having relationship issues or just plain personal problems. They would accompany me to these sessions.

* * * * *

I went to see a couple who had been having some serious marriage problems. The wife asked and the husband accepted the arrangement. When I met the couple, the first thing I noticed is that they were both very beautiful-looking people. They were also the same height.

My friend and I sat in the living room. The couple went back and forth to the kitchen a few times getting drinks (non-alcoholic) and appetizers. I could hear the husband making disparaging remarks to the wife. She would not respond to them. The tension this created was very palpable.

After an hour or so, I asked if we could talk. The couple, of course, knew my purpose beforehand. I spoke in a matter-of-fact manner. I was not accusatory. I directed my conversation to the husband. I explained that he was angry because he was not tall; however, he had everything else anyone could ask for. I explained that his wife adored him for who he was. I also said a loyal dog can be kicked one time too many, and it would be a very sorry day for him if he lost her.

Then I told him he should look at what he has, rather than what he doesn't have. I said it was completely his decision as to whether he enjoyed the gifts in his life or lived miserably asking for more. I told him he was a loving person, just stuck in a rut. I said he does deserve to be loved.

After that, I stood up and said I truly hoped he would make a decision to enjoy his gifts, one of which was his wife. I said she was definitely a keeper and he should be very thankful.

I opened my arms to him. His wife said, "Oh, no, he doesn't show affection." The husband and I met midway and embraced in a wonderful heartfelt hug. He got the message. It was a beautiful experience.

* * * * *

Another time, I was briefed on a problem a married couple were having with their fourteen-year-old son. My friend told me the son was lifting weights and had put on a lot of muscle. She explained that the parents were afraid of him because not only was he muscular, he also had terrible tantrums. She asked me if I could do anything.

We went to the home one evening. We just socialized with the parents for a while in the kitchen. The son came up from the basement and informed the parents that he and his friend were going out for a while. The parents objected for some reason or other; I've forgotten exactly why. What I witnessed next was extremely bizarre. The boy threw himself backwards, landing on the floor and halfway under the kitchen table, all the while flailing his arms and banging the floor loudly with his arms AND HIS HEAD!

I never knew what I was going to do in these "sessions." It was the spirit that was in control. I immediately threw myself down on the floor and imitated his actions. He sat up, looked at me, and then began to laugh. We all laughed with him. He never had another tantrum again.

* * * * *

The same woman who took me to this prior session arranged a meeting with a single mother of two daughters. One girl was about twelve years old, very polite and well behaved. The other daughter was about nine years old and was developmentally disabled. Her name was Lisa.

Again, being briefed beforehand, I was told that there were ongoing bitter arguments on a daily basis between Lisa and her mother. The mother was completely exhausted by these altercations. I went to the home with the woman who arranged this meeting. We sat in the kitchen talking about this and that.

Lisa and her sister entered the kitchen periodically to check with the mom for one thing or another. The first thing I noticed was that the mother spoke to her older daughter in her normal voice, but when she spoke to Lisa, her voice changed and sounded more patronizing. I could see the discomfort in Lisa's face.

About the third or fourth time Lisa came in, the mother spoke again in this patronizing voice. Lisa looked at me. It was as if she knew what I was there for; she just couldn't express it. I connected with her gaze and I felt a normal little girl trapped in a body that did not have all of its wiring properly connected.

Lisa knew something was amiss, but she didn't want to be treated differently. I became her translator. I told the mother that she must not speak to Lisa any differently than she did to her other daughter. The mother looked at me in disbelief. I then recommended that she find a therapist she felt comfortable with and begin sessions as soon as possible.

Well, three or four years later, I was in a sandwich shop in her neighborhood. Someone tapped me on the shoulder. It was the mom. She reminded me of the advice I had given her. She said after our meeting, she did find a therapist she really liked. She told the therapist what I had said. The therapist suggested she try it. She said there was no more conflict between them (at least over the patronizing voice). She thanked me for my advice. That felt so good.

* * * * *

There were quite a few of these sessions that took place over a period of a few years. All were positive experiences. It seemed as though the spirit couldn't lose. Ultimately, I had to stop doing these therapy sessions, for they started taking up quite a bit of time and I wasn't charging for them. I felt the need to devote my time to my practice of meditation.

* * * * *

I met a woman at a social gathering. She had her two little girls with her, ages six and four. I love children and it takes them two seconds to know it. We all sat on the couch together and talked and played as if we had always known one another.

I complimented the mom on her little angels. She responded that the younger one was not quite the angel I imagined. I thought that was hard to believe, given her present temperament, and asked the mother when the little girl was not an angel.

The mother told me that every morning, the child would wake up and act out. When I asked the mother how long this lasted, she told me until the little girl was dropped of at daycare.

The light went on! I cautiously suggested that there had been a time when the mother would take some time with her daughter as the little girl was waking up. When Mom had to go back to work, there was no longer time to spend together in the morning and the little girl was angry at her mother for taking Mom away.

I suggested that Mom just take a minute or two to sit on the little girl's bed as she was waking up in the morning, perhaps holding her hand or stroking her forehead. The Mom could ask if the daughter was ready to start the day with her mother.

I always feel self-conscious when a torrent of ideas pours out of me, wondering if my words are inappropriate.

Some months later, at another social gathering, the same woman approached me. She reminded me of our previous conversation and told me she had done exactly as I had suggested. She told me, "It worked like magic" and thanked me. She then shared, "I teach my students to think outside the box. You reminded me of just how important that concept is."

When I asked her what and where she taught, she told me she was a professor at an Ivy League college and taught health behavior and interventions.

* * * * *

So where do these evaluations come from? I certainly don't have the formal education in this area. They pop into my head with no time for deductive reasoning. While I am thankful for these experiences, I cannot take any credit for them personally.

My Miscellaneous Musings

Getting to know oneself is good; getting to know God is great. This God/Energy/Light cannot see, hear, touch, taste or smell except through a biological form. Our five senses are also sensed with one—awareness. Be that which senses the senses. All things in existence are in symbiotic relationships including God and man.

* * * * *

Compassion is a sign of an awakened individual.

* * * * *

You must become in love with existence/being.

We are like an arrow shot into the sky at birth. The initial trajectory is straight up. Time is like gravity forcing all things to return to the source. When the peak of the trajectory of our life is reached, the descent is not straight, but in an ever- increasing arc, downwards, to meet the earth.

There is an "aura" of light we are born with that nurtures us until we reach the apex of the height of the arrow. Then this "aura" begins to dissipate. It is before this dissipation begins, after all of our physical and mental growth has peaked, that is the best time to tap into the energy of the universe.

The creation of the universe by the Big Bang is exactly the same as our creation. It will also expand until the energy runs out and then collapses into itself. The same process holds true of the death of any star. Then the process repeats itself, forever.

* * * * *

The pinnacle achievement is the union of man and God/Light/Energy. We are a bubble of consciousness within an infinite and all-encompassing consciousness. The only thing that keeps the two from merging is the thoughts. Thoughts are a barrier between the two forms of consciousness. It's as if we were just renting space.

Take, for example, your dream state. You believe that the monster chasing you is real, or the suitor is real. In fact, you do not know what the other is going to do next. AND THIS IS YOUR DREAM! It is the same with the God/Light/

Energy consciousness. So it is that we are created in its image.

* * * * *

So, what is the difference between a musician listening to the music he/she is playing and someone simply listening to thoughts? The musician's mind is silently listening in the present moment. He/she is no longer aware of the self. The musician has merged with and actually become the music. That someone is listening internally to his or her thoughts. Get it?

You need to witness yourself. If you are outside of yourself, you are merging with the God/ Light/Energy. Inside, you are blocked off from this God/Light/Energy by the thoughts. The ego creates a jail and then keeps the soul prisoner.

* * * * *

There are higher evolved beings without physical form. Some are beings of compassion. Others are evil entities created by the collective consciousness of man. There is no opposite to God/Light/ Energy. How could there be? There is only one energy encompassing everything.

* * * * *

I cannot think of anything more intriguing than attempting to solve the mystery of my existence. I am pretty much in constant awe.

* * * * *

When the seat of your consciousness shifts, it goes outside the box. It becomes the observer. And the reason this is such a euphoric state of being is God/Light/Energy is the great and only observer. This God/Light/Energy is what looks out from your eyes. You just "think" it's you. Lifeforms, including us, are the mirror that makes it possible for the God/Light/Energy to see/realize itself. The perfection in it means we all determine our own fate.

This God/Light/Energy does not have to "judge." The rules are set up so our thoughts are our very own judge and jury. We just don't realize that when trapped within the ego.

Some people constantly complain. Every act and function becomes a burden. t does not matter how much you have. It is the very content of our minds that determines whether we live in heaven or hell and to what degree in between. What a simple and perfect master plan. If only we could learn to trust it.

* * * * *

It never abandons us—we abandon it.

* * * * *

I was watching an interview with a woman on television. She was actually diagnosed with terminal cancer. She stated she was at the end of her battle and she no longer wanted to fight. In an extremely weakened condition, she was rushed to the hospital. Her doctors gave her twenty-four to thirty-six hours to live.

In her coma, she said she went to a very beautiful place. She said she felt enormous love and compassion. She stated she felt she was with Christ himself. Then she made the following statement. "As much as I love my children, husband and family, if I had the choice, I would not have returned to this life." That's how beautiful that place was.

I knew then that her experience was authentic because that's exactly the way I felt. I was not in a coma, but I was enveloped in that beautiful light. I also felt the presence of a benevolent, all-knowing energy. This energy pervaded my being as if I were looking through an enlightened being's eyes, as if this energy tenanted my body with my permission.

This energy is actually the universal God/Light/Energy called by many names. And, this most exquisite energy is within each and every one of us.

So, to finish this story, this woman came cut of the coma and within three months was totally cancer free. This is a verifiable interview on a national television station.

* * * * *

Our thoughts expend an enormous amount of energy. We use the mind as a security blanket. We actually think the mind is what we are. We need to go beyond the mind to find our true nature of being.

* * * * *

The witness is what always was and always will be.

* * * * *

Reaching this place is the pinnacle of all human achievements.

* * * * *

* * * * *

If I ask no more questions, I will need no more answers.

* * * * *

What most consider entertainment, I now consider chaos.

* * * * *

Arrogance and ignorance go hand in hand.

* * * * *

We keep on looking for our purpose, a meaning to life. The only purpose is to be. There is no reason for being. Why does there have to be?

* * * * *

Age and death are what it takes to make us humble, and even this is sometimes not enough for some.

* * * * *

Avoid any vexations to the spirit. Do not give this negative energy a home. Protect your spirit as you would your child.

* * * * *

For those nonbelievers, all I can say is balance and form cannot be born out of chaos. In fact, there is no chaos in this universe. It just appears that way. The universe is simply in the process of creating the elements it needs to support itself and biological life. This universe is nothing less than an inordinately large hadron collider like the one located in Geneva, Switzerland.

* * * * *

If the chemical consistency of this universe were a percent of a percent to one side or another, biological life would not be capable of existence. This universe panders to the environment biological life needs to survive.

* * * * *

Ask yourself a serious question. Could this be accidental?

* * * * *

Just because the door is shown to you does not mean you will open it. Have fun, enjoy, play every game until they all appear the same and become boring. Then you will be ready to open that door.

* * * * *

The essence of what I am is that which always was and always will be. To know thy true self. The science of self is the highest science known to man.

* * * * *

There is a formula for this study. This practice involves the science of God/Light/Energy. Think of energy like money. Don't squander it. The energy we waste is like money in a drunk's hands.

If you want to experience enhancement of the senses, then quiet mind must be attained in one's youth when the sexual energy is at its peak. Unfortunately, this is when the ego/thinking mind has its greatest hold over us. As this energy is diverted from the mind to the senses, there will be a shift in consciousness.

This shift of consciousness cannot be willed or forced. It happens by itself. We simply set the stage through preparation. The few times I tried to force it proved to be very embarrassing. One must practice the energy conservation methods outlined in this book in order for this to happen.

* * * * *

This life everlasting does exist. We will not lose our sense of being in death, even the most wicked of us. The ego does fade away. There is the "essence of our being" if you will, that remains intact until our rebirth. Every parent knows a child is born with a personality making him/her an individual. Where does this personality come from...previous lifetimes perhaps?

* * * * *

Through meditation, we can re-identify with the essence of our being. Once this sensation is attained, there is no longer any fear. I believe all human beings live in a cloaked sense of abject fear. The wrathful deities in Tibetan Buddhism depict this well. This is why we continually attempt to cram as much of life activity as possible into every moment we live. We just act like everything is cool. We also act as if we are happy.

* * * * *

The only way to freedom is by studying ourselves by making science projects of ourselves. The completion we seek is right under our nose. How could anyone take this existence as anything less than an incredible miracle? To see it any other way is just too sad of a disconnect.

* * * * *

We live in a huge, limitless energy field, a consciousness, like a fabric all around us permeating everything. It is the same type of consciousness we are only it is limitless and without ego. This energy/consciousness does not judge and yet is the source of everything. The checks and balances do, however, show intent, a plan if you will.

It is my belief that there are very high forms of consciousness as depicted in all systems of belief. I believe that eventually, with their spiritual evolution, will allow themselves to merge with this unadulterated consciousness upon their sense of completion at their own will. This will also be our experience at some point in our spiritual evolution. With all of the dynamics that govern our universe, I suspect that the architecture for everything can be found in the smallest particle.

* * * * *

It is the ego that strives to create its image and seeks to constantly be entertained. This energy expenditure comes at a great cost. This energy sends out ripples into the energy field all around us. Life is the mirror of our very soul.

Thoughts do not necessarily manifest as actions. You can think about becoming the richest person in the world all you want and it will be unlikely to ever happen. The consciousness surrounding us will pick up on our core energy.

The world you manifest will derive its energy from your energy, not your thoughts. You can create all the positive thoughts you can muster, but the outside consciousness reads how you actually feel.

* * * * *

There will come a time with each and every one of us will want nothing but peace/rest/quiet. The struggle for identity begins to wane. This peace becomes more important than anything else to us. Like the pebble dropped into the calm water, this peace radiates outward into the energy around us, and reflects back to its source as well.

In this state, one feels like he/she is with a long lost and old friend. One can see the spirit within the physical world. There is a kind of mutual recognition. You recognize your being. It is that recognition that is self-fulfilling.

* * * * *

Religions use the practice of giving up one's material possessions. This makes us realize we truly don't own anything, not even this body. You can have things but they will not act as your security blanket. These things will not be your be all end all.

* * * * *

When we die, there is no loss of being. The thought process does cease. Your sense of being does not.

* * * * *

We are all far away from home—you might say lost.

* * * * *

When we are thinking, which is pretty much constant, consecutive inner dialogue if you will, we are not in touch with our surroundings. We have created a world within a world. We're cognizant that it is raining, or the birds might be singing, but we are not in touch with it. We are detached from our environment.

The inner thoughts are like a reality dream within the bigger reality dream going on outside of us. When we become one with the bigger reality we experience a bliss with this connectedness. The cosmic consciousness becomes our mind, our very self.

* * * * *

I was speaking with a young gentlemen at a gathering once. We connected on a spiritual level. He was telling me about a time he was paddling a canoe in a stream in the country by himself when he suddenly saw the landscape transform into something very surreal. He said everything seemed to come alive. He said he never experienced this phenomenon again and he would never forget it.

Such occurrences are mentioned in the different systems of belief as a religious experience, bliss, ecstasy, or rapture. This phenomenon does exist. I don't know how or why, but it does. Even if scientists explain it away as a chemical change in the brain, I don't care—it's so beautiful. I would like to ask the scientists what precipitates this phenomenon. They would probably have an answer for that as well.

* * * * *

So once the thoughts are tamed, so is the ego. They are one and the same. All thoughts serve the self/ego.

* * * * *

If you don't get to know that pure consciousness before you die, re-entering that realm will be a frightening experience for you. If you do get to know that place you will feel blissfully at home.

* * * * *

Once, a lady said to me "I think, therefore I am." And I spontaneously responded "Ahh, but will you still be without thought and, if so, what is that?"

She didn't really answer. Her body shuddered and she made some sort of unearthly sound while walking away. I knew she had just been initiated (the great teacher is within each one of us). She would never be the same person again.

* * * * *

We must give way to our own evolution. To cling to what we think we are, I call "crystalized consciousness" and leads to certain paralysis of spiritual growth.

In Tibetan Buddhism, the path to enlightenment is lined on both sides with fearful and wrathful deities. We must learn to walk past them without fear. We are the actual creators of these wrathful deities. They are our demons.

Fear will be a constant companion for this part of our spiritual journey. When the self begins to become aware of eternity, there is a natural feeling of diminution. This path requires great courage and will.

* * * * *

So, it is true what Catholics learn in catechism: "God is everywhere." We are immersed in this God/Light/Energy. It is all around us. It is consciousness. Everything is within the mind of God. It does not know that it is. It just is.

What separates us is our self-awareness. To regain the "innocence," we must lose ourselves in the moment and forget that we are!! We must just be.

All the methods to achieve this are written in parables in all the systems of belief. I would never have even considered these stories/parables would be based in actual truth. I would have thought they were just nice principles to live by.

* * * * *

* * * * *

We have to face our worst fear, our worst nightmare—silence. And we must face this with our other worst nightmare. We must face it alone. We must realize on a visceral level that "alone" is simply a perspective.

Would you ever guess that the truth is hidden in the place we fear the most—silence? We even call it "dead" silence.

The final stage of this path is to immerse yourself in it, completely and permanently. In this silence is the sounds of creation, the sounds of the consciousness of God. So, it's ok to be alone and it's ok to be silent. Why would it ever not be?

* * * * *

When a group of musicians play together, they can each feel that wonderful sense of oneness with each other. It's as intimate as love making without the sex or male/female identification. It is this taste of at-one-ment that the artist so loves especially within a group. It is the magic of the artist to pull you into this energy field. This is the attraction. We all want to go there.

The artist is able to make you feel what he/she feels—transcendence over self achieves expanded consciousness. It is true that those that seek only material wealth are the true paupers. Their spirit can never fly. The term for a truly connected musician is called trance musician. This person is one with the universal creative energy, flying far above and into the universe, sensing no fear, no boundaries and absolute freedom. I use music as an example but it is true of course for all of the arts.

Things to Think About

Do some research on the practice of attaining trance by the Kung Indians of Africa. We of our sadly intellectualized and defined culture consider their practice primitive. It is the supposedly cultured people who have lost touch. (See link: DER Documentary N_um Tchai The Ceremonial Dance of the !Kung Bushmen.htm).

This is the same energy as the "chi" so highly praised in the practice of the martial arts. It is also the same energy as Kundalini in found in yoga.

These people have a practice in which both adult men and women dance and chant for extended periods of time with no interruption. At some point, certain people will seem to pass out and lie on the ground. These people are tended to by the other tribe members.

The people lying on the ground writhe as if in pain and utter strange sounds. These people are asked questions i.e. will the spring bring good weather for a good crop or if their neighboring tribesmen deserve their trust or even who stole a certain item from the tribe. And they get answers.

Here is the practice of trance in its most primitive form used for transcending normal human limits of information.

* * * * *

A professor of anthropology at a university I was attending informed us he had just returned from Bali. He state he went there to study the natives' practice of spring rite. The ritual was performed each spring in order to gain insight into the coming weather conditions for their plantings and to connect with certain spirits to show homage. He added that he had a film that could quite possibly have a lifelong impact on the way we see the world. I was immediately intrigued.

About twenty students attended. These were the 35-millimeter days. The professor started the movie after a short introduction. I remember seeing a circle of women in the middle and men dancing around them to that unmistakable Balinese music. The professor stated the ceremony starts with the sunrise. He pointed out two girls sitting in chairs at opposite sides of the circle. He stated these young girls were not yet at the age of puberty.

The dancing, singing and music continues all day long without interruption. Toward dusk, the professor points out that the two girls are asleep with their heads drooped in the chairs. At this point, the music, singing and dancing stops. A man approaches each girl and lifts the girl onto his shoulder. Then the girls are standing on each of the men's shoulders, still asleep, still with their heads down. The men begin to walk around the circle of people as the Balinese music starts to play again.

Each of the girls begins to dance that beautiful Balinese style on the shoulders of the men, each still asleep, eyes closed. As if this is not miracle enough, they are also both dancing in perfect unison with each other and with perfect balance while on the shoulders of the men walking around the circle. I saw this film.

* * * * *

I happened to catch an ad in a local newspaper for an introduction to the power of hypnosis at a nearby college. I have always had an interest in hypnosis since it has a lot in common with meditation. I entered the auditorium where this event was to take place. The students were rather noisy, standing around and talking to each other.

A mid-thirties gentleman approached the podium. The students did not acknowledge his entrance. He waited quietly for a few minutes then suddenly spoke in a loud voice stating something like, "Please give me the next ten minutes to share with you my enthusiasm regarding hypnosis. This is a scientific study, not meant for entertainment. Then, if you have no interest, you may leave, but at least give me the next ten minutes." The audience quieted immediately and sat down. He thanked them and introduced himself. He explained that he would do an overall hypnotic suggestion to the entire audience. There were probably thirty people in the auditorium.

After some hypnotic suggestions, he was able to recognize twelve people in the audience that seemed to be in a mild hypnotic trance. He picked out six male students and six female students. After some entertaining exhibitions of his proficiency in hypnosis, he took all of the subjects out of trance and sent them back to their seats with the exception of one female student.

This is where things became interesting. First he stated to the student that she was in love with him. She walked up to him and threw her arms around his neck and expressed a glowing smile. He looked at the audience and said this should answer your question as to why anyone would want to become a hypnotist.

There was a very strong humorous and positive response from the audience. The hypnotist now commanded the complete attention of the audience. He then asked the female student how old she was and what year in college she was in. She responded that she was in her freshman year and she stated her age. The hypnotist asked her to sign her name on the chalkboard, which she did.

He then asked her if she remembered her senior year in high school. She replied that she did. He asked her to recall her graduation ceremonies. He again asked her to sign her name on the chalkboard. This time her signature appeared more neatly written. The hypnotist asked the student to go back to her ninth grade junior high school` year.

He again asked her if she remembered her graduation ceremonies. She replied that she did. He asked her to sign her name on the chalkboard. Now her signature was much more neatly written than in the previous two. And there was an additional anomaly; her voice was now that of an adolescent. The hypnotist continued to bring the student to earlier times in her life, in fact, right back to the first grade.

He asked her if she remembered going to school for that first day. She responded affirmatively. She wrote her name on the chalkboard. This took quite some time. It was in printed form. Her voice was that of a little girl. She was adorable.

The hypnotist released her from the trance, thanked her and stated she could take her seat. He explained to the audience that this was known as somnambulism. He stated his interest in hypnotism centered on what is called "age regression". He stated there are certain subjects that exhibit the ability to enter previous lifetimes. He stated studies on these subjects show proof they know nothing about the environment of these previous lifetimes while in their present ones. Yet, while under hypnotic trance, they can speak foreign languages complete with appropriate accents. They mention dates and people of this past time that can be verified through historical records.

* * * * *

I saw an ad in another local newspaper "Japanese sword master demonstrates his art." The demonstration was held at a school. I was surprised to find the seating was practically filled. The audience seated themselves and then settled down. As if on cue, the curtains opened.

A student gave some background on the Zen school and the teacher. He then introduced his teacher as he came out to the stage. The teacher did not speak English. The narrator explained that the teacher would be blindfolded, then he would cut watermelons placed on the stomachs of three students laying on the floor, one in front and one on either side of the teacher.

The students lay down and other students placed the watermelons on their stomachs. The master kneeled in the back of the stage with the three students in front and both sides of him. Two of the other students proceeded to blindfold him. There was a lamp on the stage. The students held a black cloth in front of the light to show the audience it was opaque. They then wrapped this around the head of the master. Then they placed a black face mask in front of the light. Again, no light shined through. This mask was placed on the master.

Then the students held a heavy and long cloth hood in front of the light. It appeared to be opaque as well. This hood was then placed on the master. If this was a trick, it was a damn good one. The students then stepped to the perimeter of the stage. All became quiet.

The master just sat there for what seemed like ten minutes but was probably five. He then jumped to his feet, swung to his left and cut the watermelon right in half on this student, then he turned in the opposite direction and cut the watermelon on the second students stomach and without any break in time, he threw himself to his knees while sliding to the front student and cut this watermelon in half as well. I was only about twenty years old (before my light experience) at the time. I was profoundly impressed with this humanly impossible act.

* * * * *

In my later years, I became a reef tank hobbyist. I learned so much about life and people from watching the fish and invertebrates in this tank. All the inhabitants were interdependent on each other. There were wonderful symbiotic relationships. I realized that the anemones, even though did not have eyes, seemed to know where the confines of the tank were and where the different rock formations were as well. They used this sense to move around the tank when they chose to. It made me think about the Zen sword master. Had he developed an additional sense through his practice of Zen?

Meanderings to Consider

Inspiration is creative energy. The people that seek to acquire more and more of the material world expend large amounts of energy doing so. This effort robs the spirit and body of precious energy causing physical and mental illnesses. Creative energy possesses you and courses through your being like a river of light passing through you. Of course, this light is healing. It is the creative energy of all that there is. It is the Creator. It is effortless to live when one is inspired. As it is said "when the Spirit moves you" is absolutely true.

* * * * *

Following the path of meditation is strictly an intuitive process. It is a natural instinct within each one of us. The intellect is actually the biggest impediment to progress. There will come a time when your inner universe becomes much more fascinating than the outer one. When we are thinking, we are not in touch with our environment. We may be cognizant that it is raining, but we are not one with it. We create a world within a world, detaching ourselves from the source of energy. When we are connected to this wellspring of energy, we can experience bliss. There is a union between the soul and God. The process of meditation will bring you to a point of experiencing wonder over what you are and "that you are". This wonder spills over to everything in the universe. You become that child again.

* * * * *

My struggle with fitting in loses its hold on me more and more with each day. I can finally say, at the age of sixty-seven, I no longer suffer with this need. The struggle to "fit in" was one of my greatest challenges, because I didn't "fit in". I didn't belong at parties or night clubs. But I didn't know what else to do with myself during my youth. I tried to suppress my spiritual longing. But this didn't work.

I saw everyone being controlled by the creative energy the same way all living creatures are. There was no difference. People became mesmerized by this energy, in a trance, drugged by hormones, all for the purpose of procreation and survival. Some people live and survive in a symbiotic manner. But most live as predators in a parasitic way. People as a whole do not see who you are. They see their own needs, they see what they want and need to see.

* * * * *

In my early thirties, I asked a friend why he thought sex felt good. He answered, do you have to question everything? It made me realize that I have always questioned everything.

* * * * *

In my late twenties, I had my astrological chart done by a very well-known astrologer in my area. She told me my chart had something very unique about it. Of course I asked what. She said my chart showed three triangles superposed over one another. She said that was the sign of a mystic.

* * * * *

The mind is the most powerful computer there is. It dominates and controls us. It is the master. When this servant is tamed we become the true master. The witness can be found in the center of the hurricane of thoughts. It is still, it is calm. It expends no energy. It just is. If you reach this state of consciousness, you will have attained the pinnacle of human achievements.

* * * * *

Balance and form cannot be a product of chaos. In fact, what we define as chaos is actually part of the mechanisms of the universe that maintain this very delicate balance and form.

* * * * *

There are beings that figured it all out long ago. The answer can never be discovered by the intellect. For the intellect will achieve an answer for every one of it's questions, the problem is that answer will then create another question and so ad infinitum, because there is no end. Following the path is strictly an intuitive process. One cannot know the answer, one must become IT.

* * * * *

I do not believe it is necessary to achieve the experience of Kundalini for total realization. Kundalini can only be achieved when the sexual/ creative energy is at its peak. Although this is truly an experience beyond words, so is the achieve-ment of absolute inner quiet/peace. This gift is available at any age throughout life. The practitio-ner can play with the energy. One's body in the normal mode is like running a vehicle on regular gas.

One's body on Kundalini energy is like running on high octane racing fuel. This causes the body and mind to run on a much higher capacity. Perfect pitch, enhanced vision and physical strength is achieved as well as psychic abilities. Again, this must be practiced in your youth in order to tap into the energy when it is at its peak. Of course all of these enhanced abilities were enjoyed immensely.

The pinnacle of achievements is to slay the monster racing mind and experience quiet, peace of mind/being. You will still grow old, you will still wither away, and you will eventually lose this energy. You will never loose the connection even in the death of the body. You will embrace death because you will know what you are to become. You will unite with your true self once again. The true self has no identity. This is like coming home after a very long absence.

* * * * *

So, believe it or not, you don't have to be chaste and holy to pursue this path. The practice itself will cleanse your spirit. It is possible for a death row inmate to have an epiphany. After this experience this person will no longer be the same. The resulting compassion and conscience attained with these experiences come from that same universal origin.

* * * * *

When the mind finally wishes for nothing but peace it will come to rest. You must want this more than anything else. Only then will your inner spirit merge with the outer spirit, God/Light/ Energy. The practice of meditation is truly the only method there is to slay the ego by mastering it. We must exercise our will to regain our ability to just be. We practice meditation to purify our mind of thoughts of self. The will is the only thing stronger than the want.

Once the mind is tamed, one attains the mastery. You become thee master, and there is only one. You will find yourself in the Garden of Eden. 'Birds singing, clouds in wonderful and ever changing forms, the breezes caress and the quiet becomes your sense of the infinite universe all around you. You can feel it. You can feel eternity. Think of this place as a parallel universe floating right alongside this one. Once we harmonize our vibration with it, we will merge with it! The only way to get inner peace is to give it to yourself. No harm can come to you for you will not harm yourself. There is truth to the story of Daniel in the lion's den. This is when the lion will lie with the lamb.

* * * * *

If we look at children, their pastime is to play, sleep and eat. Animals want to play, sleep and eat. Simple. We spend far more energy than we produce working for the almighty dollar. We sell our health for a dollar bill. We operate at an energy deficit. We sell our souls. This lifestyle is entirely fear based. No wonder most people are miserable. But, the people who play...music, dancing, painting, etc., they are happy and content. If we change our perspective from one word, work, to another, play, our lives will be much happier and fulfilled.

* * * * *

The children of the world have been placed in our charge. They learn, like all species, by copying the actions of their caregivers. Certainly they enter this world with some hardwiring for survival. I believe some of the children's behaviors are also hardwired from their parents. So the parent's issues become born again. If a parent is preju-diced, then it is likely the child will be as well. Other caregivers in this child's life could counteract this negative trait. We can't, in good conscience, say this is none of our business. If we could only take the responsibility for this programming seriously, we could engender positive traits for future generations while discouraging any negative ones.

People could become more altruistic and socially responsible. Why can't we understand greed is an anti-social behavior. We are capable of making this world a better place by working on ourselves, sharing our lessons and spreading the love.

* * * * *

I was talking to a doc family member on the phone. He expressed to me that he felt completely stressed out. He said he was always rushing from one place to another. He stated there was never enough time. This person is retired and a millionaire to boot.

I said, "Shovel the poop and be happy you have the physical ability to do so."

He said, "So change my perspective."

I said, "Yes, it's a choice."

We have to diligently watch our thoughts. They control the chemistry of our bodies just like any medication.

* * * * *

It's all self-adornment—the house, the job, even the family. It's a reflection of yourself created by you. We all want to show who we are to others by what we surround ourselves with. It's all about image. The false God we worship is US!

Taking care of the immediate family is an extension of the ego. Taking care of the family of man is an extension of the compassionate one.

* * * * *

I don't feel any more special than anybody else. I'm just an ordinary person who had an extraordinary experience. I recently said to someone that I've simply gone off the deep end. But I live with these memories/experiences. They were real. One minute I was regular me and then the next minute I was witnessing indescribable beauty/heaven. I do know this sounds crazy. Because I've seen these things with my own eyes, I can't deny these things happened to me.

Every culture has its own belief system but I believe they are all based on the same phenomenon. Certain individuals have transcendental experiences. Sometimes these experiences are witnessed by others. When these experiences are put down in writing, there is always hyperbole in order to impress the populace. Unfortunately, for some, this hyperbole diminishes the veracity of these events. Each culture believes their way is the only way. Each culture has its own collective ego.

* * * * *

The tenet of life everlasting can only be found when individuals discover that center of their being, the witness, calmful watcher or the third eye. The part of the self that is the ego does fade away. Meditation emulates the process of death. You will forget your status in life, your name and even your sexuality. You will become pure spirit again. Anyone can experience or sense that pure spirit before death occurs. The essence of our being is pure spirit = God/Light/Energy. This is the realization of life everlasting. We always were and we always will be. Only when an individual experiences this essence will all doubts be removed. It is the ego alone that separates us from God. It's that simple.

* * * * *

When you arrive at the center of the cyclone, you will know it. One of the symptoms is you will not want to leave. We desperately need this place of regeneration.

The witness/calmful watcher/third eye is in the center of the cyclone of thoughts. It is that still, calm, core of all activity. This is the place where we truly reside.

* * * * *

Don't wait 'til death to rest in peace.

* * * * *

When it is said that we are created in his image, what does that mean? God certainly does not have a physical body. When you are dreaming, you think that monster chasing you or the suitor across the table is real. You also don't know what is going to happen next do you? When you are awake, you realize that you created these entities. These entities had free will in your dream did they not? This is why we all have free will. God's mind is the same as ours. This is why man is the microcosm of the macrocosm. We are a small sphere of consciousness within a limitless consciousness of God/Light/Energy.

This energy field just is. It has no sense of self. This single form of energy was split into two equal parts, positive and negative, yin and yang. And, this single form of energy must always find a way to balance the positive and negative perfectly. I do believe the God/Light/Energy does have intent. There is definitely a master plan.

* * * * *

Just remember that every time you are feeling bad for yourself that it was you that made that choice.

* * * * *

We need to stop wanting. We need to look at what we have and not what we don't have.

When trance musicians like Coltrane or Dolphy played they did not make any effort. The spirit (the only spirit) plays and the musician listens. Nureyev was also a trance performer. A very accomplished musician I know was asked how he remembers "all of those notes." He really did not know how to answer this question.

The answer is he does not remember "all of those notes." He/she is hearing them for the first time, since it is the spirit that is actually playing. A true artist does not know what he/she is going to do next. Their inventions are a spontaneous act. You think you are watching the performer. The performer is God/Light/Energy using the human body. The human performer is just the witness. This is how living life itself should be done.

This is when you are in the moment! The cluttered and rushing thoughts stop. Our greatest joy is found in just being.

* * * * *

Every moment rushed is a moment lost.

* * * * *

Once we give up trying to figure it all out, once we stop trying to define everything, it just comes to us. We are allowed to enter this place of indescribable beauty when we lose about ninety percent of our ego.

* * * * *

I met a woman and we immediately connected on a spiritual level. She stated she was Muslim. I commented that the Muslim religion was a very beautiful belief system. She told me she had recently gone to her country, where she had not been since she was a child. She told me how connected she felt to be with her family members even though she didn't remember them. She then told me that she learned it was okay to be silent for periods of time in the group. There was no discomfort with the group in silence as there is in America.

* * * * *

How is it that all cultures have pretty much the same religious stories consisting of a heaven and a hell?

* * * * *

The great spiritual leaders of the world—Jesus, Buddha, Mohamed, Moses—and the great freedom fighters—Gandhi, Nelson Mandela and Martin Luther King—are all messengers of the one Great Spirit. These people were all driven by the same universal Energy/Light/God.

* * * * *

We can never comprehend God intellectually. That would be like trying to fit the ocean into a drop of water. We can, however, merge with this Energy/Light/God while still retaining a sense of ourselves.

On Love

I t's easy to mistake chemistry for love. Sexual attraction is clearly not love. This is the legerdemain of nature showing you that you will both make healthy babies. It's nature's trick to get you to procreate. You may not even be emotionally and psychologically compatible. But the drugging of your mind and body with hormones and chemicals makes us blind to that. It still may be possible to develop a good, successful and long lasting relationship. The chemistry of sexual attraction must evolve into a "best friends for life" scenario. Two loving people will share a loving relationship.

Bonding between people promotes a sense of wellbeing. What we call love is actually the same state of euphoria experienced by the artists and anyone else that uses a method to access at-one-ment. The experience of parenting provides this sense of oneness. Caring for animals and plants will also provide this state of at-one-ment. A person laying a stone wall or sweeping a floor who is completely in the moment can access this state as well. This state of at-one-ment is like brushing against the veil that separates heaven and earth.

You have to love the whole picture. You can't love just part of it. That is conditional love. Loving the whole picture is unconditional love/compassion. That is only possible by the compassionate being which can manifest in each one of us.

With this practice of meditation, the centers will come alive with their new source of energy to operate on. When the heart center opens you will experience this unconditional love. The practice of Yoga clearly defines all of the centers. Catholicism depicts Christ pointing to his heart with his right hand and to heaven with his left. This is that same opening up of the heart center taught in Yoga. Why shouldn't all of the belief systems be in sync? We all come from the same seed.

When I was twenty-five years old, I went to see a Zen master. When I sat down, he asked me who I was and where I came from. I answered that I did not know who I was or where I came from. I just discovered I was here. He smiled and said "you will make it." I said I came to ask one question. "What about love?"

He answered "What do you think"?

I bowed and thanked him before leaving. He wrote a monthly editorial. That month, he mentioned how important the "I do not know mind" is. He was a source of the one and only truth. This is what I suspected. Love is not for any one thing. That is conditional love which depends on your ego. Compassion will take its place. You begin to feel this compassion for everything, every creature, every person, even ones that have made themselves your enemy. Love is only what you think, compassion is one of the laws of the universe.

Pearls of Wisdom / Aphorisms / Stories to Ponder & a Pun

Here are some wise old sayings I have always treasured. They are probably not verbatim, but close enough so you will get the general idea.

* * * * *

Before enlightenment, carry your buckets of water and armfuls of firewood. After enlightenment, carry your buckets of water and armfuls of firewood.

* * * * *

A farmer lay in bed one evening and prayed to God to grant him a genie who would do his bidding. Taking care of the farm and his family was burdensome work. The farmer prayed so earnestly, God could not refuse him. God finally granted this man his wish but with one caveat. There was one condition the man must accept in order to be awarded this genie and that condition was he must always keep the genie busy.

If the man did not keep the genie busy, the genie could get very angry and kill him! The man eagerly agreed.

The next morning, the man woke and when he looked into his backyard, he saw the genie waiting. What he thought was just a dream turned out to be real. Now he could direct the genie to perform any and all the tasks he wished, so he could have some time to himself.

He began giving orders to the genie, e.g., plow the fields, clean the troughs, paint the house, etc. The genie quickly performed these tasks. The farmer started to have to invent tasks to keep the genie busy, remembering his agreement to keep the genie busy or fear being killed. As he ran out of ideas to keep the genie busy, he began losing sleep. He would see the genie waiting in his backyard, sweating profusely.

The man became so distraught that he pleaded desperately with God to help him once again. God, with all of his compassion, could not ignore the farmer's entreaty. God instructed the farmer to order the genie to climb up and down the flagpole all night, which he anxiously did.

Then, as the farmer lay in bed, he could hear the genie climbing up and down the flagpole. The sound this was making was exactly like hearing himself breathe—up was the inhale, down was the exhale. This sound quickly lulled the farmer to a very blissful night's sleep.

Of course, the genie represents our minds and the climbing the flagpole represents repetition of prayer or mantra to slow down this extremely powerful bio-computer, so it will not get out of control.

* * * * *

A man was walking through the woods when he heard a faint call from a nearby field. As he followed the calling, he soon recognized it as a call for help. He came upon a hole from an abandoned well to find a man had fallen in and was now trapped. The trapped man was expressing his delight that someone finally showed up to save him. The man at the top of the well asked the trapped man if he was to save him, would he give his word that he would save twelve others.

The trapped man questioned him asking what kind of man was he to negotiate with someone in his position. The man at the top of the well said he was just keeping his promise to the person that saved him when he was in a similar plight.

* * * * *

An aspirant decided he would go up into the mountains, find a cave, and not leave 'til he had attained enlightenment. So, he gathered his meager belongings and set out to find his retreat. He set himself up in a small cave high up on the mountainside, a place he was certain he would not be disturbed. Even his sister, who brought him provisions regularly, did not disturb him.

There, he meditated constantly, breaking only for the sustenance necessary to keep him in good health. Years passed but his determination was steadfast. One day, he experienced a flash of light in his head. With this light, he was transformed. He felt completely filled with joy. He raced out of the cave and down the mountainside towards town so he could share his experience with everybody.

As he descended the mountainside, he came across a group of children playing. He greeted them cheerfully with his new-found transformation. The children reacted in fear throwing stones at him. He did not realize that all those years of not cutting his hair or fingernails made him a dreadful sight. He became angry with the children and began throwing stones back at them.

The lesson here, of course, is enlightenment is found in the marketplace.

* * * * *

One night, a thief broke into what he thought was a church. As he was taking some of the valuable artifacts, an old man came up to him to ask him what he was doing. The thief drew his knife and killed the old man, then promptly made his escape. It turns out that this was a school for teaching the art of samurai sword.

The students woke to find the master lying dead on the floor. It was the first student's duty to defend the honor of the master. He set out to track the thief down.

After several days, the first student was able to corner the thief in an area surrounded by mountains. The only way out for the thief was to turn around and pass by the first student. The thief knew his fate of death was certainly sealed. He walked up to the first student defiantly. The first student drew his sword and just as he began to bring it down on the thief, the thief spat in his face. The first student stopped his movement and placed his sword back in the scabbard. He turned around and began to walk away.

The thief, thoroughly befuddled, ran up beside the first student and asked, "You had the chance to kill me. Why didn't you?"

The first student replied, "Because I became angry."

* * * * *

In Africa, all the animals will drink from the same water source—river, pond or lake. This includes predator and prey alike. The wild boar is known to have a very cantankerous temperament. The wild boar will act aggressively towards the water buffalo to establish its drinking spot. Even though the water buffalo is the larger and stronger animal, it will simply retreat and find another place to drink. This is because the water buffalo is also the more intelligent animal. It realizes that a confrontation is not worth the expenditure of energy so precious in this environment.

* * * * *

Fear the tiger long enough and the tiger will appear.

* * * * *

What does a pickpocket see when he meets a saint?

* * * * *

And one of my favorites...I strongly hesitated to include this for fear some would see me only as a Christian or Catholic, is the 23rd Psalm. I know that these precepts are universal. They are found in every belief system, just worded in a slightly different way. I didn't analyze this psalm; it's true meaning just dawned on me one day. It is not a prayer; it's a set of instructions from a mystic to seekers on the path. These precepts are written in parable so as to reach two groups of people—the true seekers and the populace.

* * * * *

The LORD is my shepherd; I shall not want.

We live constantly looking around the next corner for something to fulfill us, to fill that empty space inside. This causes us to be in the fight-or-flight mode, continuously from living in this fear-based state of insecurity. This high-adrenaline state of being poisons our bodies and causes our minds to be in constant chaos. We must come to realize that everything we want is right here, right now. Work will become play and "stuff" will come and go.

He maketh me to lie down in green pastures,
He leadeth me beside the still waters,

Only when the mind is capable of complete silence can the true beauty of creation be seen. This complete silence results in complete inner peace.

He restoreth my soul,

The precious life energy is no longer squandered. Instead of being spent, it is redirected inwards which, as stated, restores the soul, body and mind.

He leadeth me in the paths of righteousness for his name's sake,

Once it is realized that everything is conscious and this consciousness is God, you realize everything is the self. The witness is this limitless consciousness/God recording our actions for the record. Once this fact is realized, it's as if everything we do is witnessed—because it is!

Yea, though I walk through the valley of the shadow of death,
I will fear no evil: for thou art with me,
Thy rod and thy staff they comfort me,

Fear will be the constant companion of all seekers on the path until it suddenly loses it's grip on us. It will cease to be by itself. The fear is caused by our sense of insignificance and helplessness in comparison to eternity. There will come a time when all seekers simply become tired of fear. When this fear loses it's grip, the seeker will be in a very restful place.

Thou preparest a table before me in the presence of mine enemies

I believe this table means your needs will be met even when you are surrounded by threatening situations. Once this deep inner state of inner peace is attained, it cannot be disturbed.

Thou anointest my head with oil,
The seeker will feel cared for.
My cup runneth over.

A great sense of fulfillment will be the constant state of mind/spirit the enlightened one will feel.

Surely goodness and mercy shall follow me all the days of my life

This sense of fulfillment will never fade.

And I will dwell in the house of the LORD forever.

Enlightenment is eternal.

Writings

Mission

Your mission undertaken with
each new day
a stair closer to your alter
bent to receive
Knowing the thoughts of self
liken unto a corpse of shadow
dripping ever close behind this spirit
in the decomposing darkness
seeking to leach on your holy body
Wanting to run but fearing to trip in haste
yet knowing the path
as you set up markers of light
ever so subtle
like the prism of colors
emerging from a dewdrop
in the early morn
making the way clear
shown only to seekers

Rhythm

You that determine the rhythm of the
of the crickets and peep frogs
chanting
You that regulate the ocean's waves
And you
breathing for me while I am yet unaware
I seek thee
From the one seed you've created
you've created many
without end
all mixing like ingredients
separated and mixed again
to watch what will become
Seeds thrown into the wind
to be carried for the expression of energy
No matter how far apart they land
a silver cord of sunlight
attached to you
Could it be the momentum
that prevents the stillness

Seeing God

I saw God today
He was right across the street
In the field the farmer owns
He was in the form of a young sheep
Jumping and running and prancing
With the joy of life
He would munch on some grass
Then suddenly spring up as if
the very ground he was on electrocuted
him
He then ran over to the older sheep,
circling, teasing, trying to entice it to play
but to no avail
He would then run like a deer back to his
spot
Sheer joy of being, no sense of self
Reminding me to play,
I saw God today

Poem to my Sister

Once
in a dream like now
where nothing is what it seems to be
yet every answer is hidden
Outside
You found your garden in the night
barren and dry
responsible for your plight
you blame this picture in your sight
like one long lost and never found
part of you you never knew
A saving grace you say
a friendly frog could save the day
Feeling your face smile
Something good in this garden after all
This garden needs your tending

Koans

Define yourself
 what are you

- - - - - - - - - - - - - - - - - - - -

Fantasizing
 in a dream
 wake up

- - - - - - - - - - - - - - - - - - - -

When it becomes quiet
 inside
 we will find
 what we've been
 looking for
 emptiness
 will be full

- -

Experiencing our sense
 of feeling
 to it's fullest
 aware of eternity

- -

Twinkle twinkle little star
 how I wonder
 what I am
If I have no more questions
 I will need no more answers

Aware of each breath
 method to develop concentration
 practice practice practice

Faced with annihilation
 in a maze
 why not look for
 a way out

Self exploration
 making a science
 of studying
 what I am
 by observing

In touch with the
 spirit inside
 in touch with the
 spirit outside

Love for something
  is finite
  Love , in and of itself
  is infinite

Death will not come to my door
  I will go to it

Always trying to create
  reality
  always trying to
  be in control

Thoughts
  ego
  separate
  suffering

If I wanted enlightenment
  for you
  It would be because
  I would be separate
  from you
  I am not separate
  from you
  or enlightenment

God is what I am
When I am not

The only path to Heaven
is through Hell

God is asleep inside of us
The only way to wake him
Is to be totally quiet

Embrace the silence
It is our birthplace

Eternity stretches out all around me

Youth and wisdom
The two great gifts in life
Unfortunately
Not to be had
        At the same time

And Finally...

We have all learned to identify with the thought processes of our minds. Those thought processes are largely imprints from our environment throughout our lives. We have not dared to venture outside out those confines. This has prevented our spiritual growth.

When this growth stops, so does our ability to "become a child again." We must resume our inner exploration. We are energy within energy, consciousness within consciousness.

Once we reconnect with that larger part of ourselves, it will speak to us, not in words but in flashes of intuitive images and impressions giving unmistakable meaning to their intent. To access this source of esoteric knowledge, we must stop expending our energy looking outwards for our completion.

We must stop looking around each and every corner for something that we think may make us happy. We must stop seeing what we don't have and look at what we have. Human beings have a rapacious appetite for "more" to fill that empty space within.

It has been a difficult task to try to put into words that which is inconceivable. The one most important point I am trying to convey is total inner peace is possible if you so choose. It's not about discipline; it's about wanting complete inner peace from the very core of our being. We must be determined to live our lives in peace. And if anything pushes us off this lofty perch, let it be our teacher.

Peace is the only point from which real love/compassion can manifest. So, peace should be our primary goal in life. This inner peace will spread into the universe like the ripples from a pebble dropped in calm water.

To look into the eye of God is to unite with that energy. And yes, your ego will die, you will not. We are surrounded by eternity. Everything is a miracle. We are a miracle, beyond the comprehension of the mind, but not beyond the comprehension of the heart.

So, I wish peace for each and every one of you. From this, unconditional love and compassion will grow. This will result in the realization that all the peoples of the world are truly one family.

Peace and Love to you all my family,
The Layman

About the Title and
Cover of this Book

I could have titled this book *THE ANSWER TO THE RIDDLE, THE DIRECT PATH, THE SECRET TO ENLIGHTENMENT, GLIMPSES OF GOD*, or *AN AMERICAN MYSTIC*.

When I was about thirty-five, I remember having a conversation with an artist/teacher. I was explaining some of my discoveries and theories to him. He replied at one point, "Ah, a universal doctrine." I knew, at that point, that would be the title of this work.

Not until I was almost done with this writing did I receive the image on the book's cover. That image came to me while I was lying down resting. It popped into my head fully intact as it presently appears. Ask yourself where did that image come from? That image shows our energy spreading out into the universe. The universe mirrors this energy back to us over a period of time. So, even if we've "cleaned up our act," there's some old energy we sent out long ago that is on its way back to us.

This is how the principle of "you reap what you sow" and the doctrine of karma actually work. Keep in mind, it's not the thoughts we must change, it's that which creates the thoughts, our core energy. This is what always was and always will be. This is what we need to reconnect with.

If you so desire and for more information,
please contact the author at

Website: https://theuniversaldoctrine.com
Email: theuniversaldoctrine@gmail.com

www.ingramcontent.com/pod-product-compliance
Lightning Source LLC
LaVergne TN
LVHW011236080426
835509LV00005B/520